The Journey toward Freedom

The Journey toward Freedom

Economic Structures and Theological Perspectives

Paul G. King *and* David O. Woodyard

Rutherford • *Madison* • *Teaneck*
Fairleigh Dickinson University Press
London and Toronto: Associated University Presses

© 1982 by Associated University Presses, Inc.

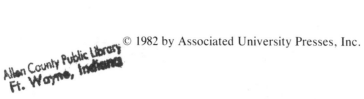
Associated University Presses, Inc.
4 Cornwall Drive
East Brunswick, N.J. 08816

Associated University Presses Ltd
27 Chancery Lane
London WC2A 1NF, England

Associated University Presses
Toronto M5E 1A7, Canada

Library of Congress Cataloging in Publication Data

King, Paul G., 1940–
   The journey toward freedom.

   Bibliography: p.
   Includes index.
   1. Liberation theology. 2. Religion and economics.
I. Woodyard, David O. II. Title.
BT83.57.K49   261.8'5'0973   81-65869
ISBN 0-8386-3115-0   AACR2

PRINTED IN THE UNITED STATES OF AMERICA

To our wives, for the gift of space,
and our children, for the gift of distraction

Contents

Introduction

The convergence of a theologian and an economist for the creation of a book is not an event that readily explains itself. Yet the explanation is almost too simple to be believable in an age where the authority of the complex prevails. We happened to be seated next to each other in the lunchroom of the college union, and the economist asked the theologian, "Does anyone in your department read liberation theology?"

The theologian had written an earlier book on liberation theology that was, in part, an effort to understand theologically his experiences in the 1960s. He anticipated writing another book, but had not yet determined its exact form, although he felt a growing conviction that liberation theology in North America needed an alliance with the social sciences in order to fulfill its destiny. That would call for capabilities few, if any, theologians possess.

The economist had just returned from a semester's leave at Oak Ridge National Laboratory. While there, he had attended a course introducing liberation theology taught by a local priest. Centered in the Third World where the economist's interests lay, the course provided a missing element in his economic analysis of Latin America. It had always been clear that development economists must address the plight of the poor, but the key to bringing about change was hidden. Liberation theology brought it into view.

The next fall we taught a course together—"The Human Condition: Economic Factors and Theological Perspectives." The emphasis was on Latin America, but a closing thrust highlighted some of the problems of social and economic change called for in the United States by the biblical tradition. Unfortunately, not much literature was available in which theological and social science themes in North America were related. That eventually led to the task of writing papers for professional meetings and then to the book at hand.

It is substantially easier to explain how an economist and a theologian found each other than to explain why we have continued to pursue joint ventures and completed a manuscript. This book is more of a dialogue than a synthesis of two disciplines. The following chapters are the result of an encounter that has created sensitivity to the contributions and the boundaries of two fields, but it is certainly not a marriage of two disciplines. It is, at best, the beginning of an integration of the specific interests of a humanist and a social scientist.

There are no definitive patterns here for others to follow, but there is a clear model that governs this work. Theology is agenda setting for the economist; economics enables the theologian to grasp why things are as they are in the social order. Theology can point the economist toward situations that call for explanation and relief and can create a sense of urgency to address these troubling situations. Economics can tell the theologian what it would take to move in the direction of an alternative vision. Liberation theology cannot fully perform its tasks without the aid of the economist, and the economist is the prisoner of the present without the haunting vision of "what ought to be" that overrides the tendency simply to accept "what is." The theologian calls before the economist the priority of the "journey toward freedom." The economist can identify what is blocking that journey and what changes are needed to move decisively toward "a new heaven and a new earth." Each needs the other. That abiding sense holds the two disciplines together in dialogue, but it has not yet yielded a complex system of integration.

It may be difficult to grasp fully a short version of a

book's thesis, but a preview of our argument may help the reader.

One of the features of liberation theology is that it comes into being where persons are getting hurt, not in air-conditioned libraries. The crucible of human existence is the setting from which one appeals to the content of the Christian tradition. Initially, the anguish of an undernourished child has more authority than Augustine. Theology must equip us not only to understand a world in which children starve in the midst of waste, but also to change that world. Proofs for the existence of God, exploration of the relationships within the Trinity, or speculation about the connection of love and justice are not appropriate points of departure. They have their place, but they only come into play when evoked by a demand to explain human experience in the world. One of the necessary tools for liberation theology is that of story—the gathering in of our experience through narrative. When the black congregation asks if the preacher "can tell the story," they want to know if he can bring the biblical story into focus with the story they are living. All of us live in and through stories, our own and those which purport to explain us. Stories keep us close to what is happening to us; they can also change us. Stories lay claim to our experience in the social order; they can change that realm as well. Liberation theology is an attempt to engage our private and our public lives through the stories of what God is doing about our journey toward freedom.

It is rare to find economists who invoke the category of "story." Theoretical analysis is their media and quantitative data their resource, but the absence of the word does not assure us that the notion is missing. As social scientists, many economists pride themselves on being "value free." In fact, what that often means is the freedom to ignore values. The economist may not be like the black preacher in being called upon to "tell the story," but an untold story is usually present and pervasive. Whether one is talking about the success of the individual in the economic order or the way in which that order works, there is an underlying narrative. The models and analyses of the economist serve as bases for stories that purport to tell us how well our system works and what benefits flow to us from it. The system and its institutions are built upon and legitimated by stories told and untold. One does not have to scratch the surface of our economic order very deeply to reveal a frontier mentality that sustains the image of America as the "land of opportunity." Opportunity and potential are crucial features of the story men and women live in the economic realm. While poverty, racism, and sexism may refute the story, it remains unchanged by the data. One *can* live a story that isn't true. Of course, the arrangements and organizations of our society ride on the narratives carrying the values of achievement, individual initiative, the free market, and economic rewards. The economist does indeed have "a story to tell the nation." Usually, that story is not about people getting hurt.

The American people embrace a national story that links our freedom saga with what God is doing. As much as any other nation in the world, America has focused upon freedom and utilized biblical symbols to express what we are about. The sense that we are a "chosen people" explains our origins and our destiny as well as our performance at the moment. We remind ourselves of that by embossing "in God we trust" on our coins and inserting "one nation under God" in our pledge of allegiance. Most Americans are convinced that we square nicely with what God is about in the world. This story reflects a civil religion rather than a biblical faith. It enables us to intensify our confidence and welds us into a sense of the whole; peoplehood emerges from a civil religion. But at the same time it serves as an "ideological screen" that prevents our coming to terms with the notion that the American Dream may be either fallen or unfulfilled—or both. A nation confident that God is on its side is an unlikely candidate for rigorous self-scrutiny. We can even find ourselves believing Richard Nixon when he said that Vietnam was our finest hour in that Americans have never done more for others with less to gain for themselves. The story behind civil religion is one of national innocence; utopia has been implemented. Our journey toward freedom is an act of self-congratulation that blinds us to those who are getting hurt.

Economists function with the equivalent of a civil religion. They have a responsibility to describe and explain the economic system. One of the most familiar and pervasive descriptions for Americans is found in the neoclassical model of the competitive economy. It gives rise to a story about economic behavior that leads us to believe that the conditions and outcomes of the model actually prevail in our world. At the center of the narrative is the notion of the market as an agent susceptible to the initiatives of the consumer. If we "let the market work," resources will be appropriately allocated and societal welfare at large will be achieved. The best interests of all will be served by the competitive actions of individuals. Consumers have choices in this story, and their decisions have appropriate consequences. Persons get what they want—and what they deserve. Whenever an apparent flaw develops in this beneficent structure, the model is amended, but the story remains intact. Thus, in the 1930s, it was suggested that government policy might allow intervention to enable the market to work once again for the common good. The problem with this neoclassical story and its revisions is that it only works for some. The market is not responsive to those who are without power in the economic order and those who suffer deprivation. It is not a facilitator of the journey toward freedom for those who need freedom most. It serves to hold in place the advantages of the advantaged and the disadvantages of the disadvantaged.

However, were we to acknowledge the priority of another version of reality than the one that prevails, the question arises as to where change must begin. The common wisdom in the land seems to be that we begin by changing persons. When Billy Graham was asked if he had ever used his relationship with Richard Nixon to talk about civil rights, Vietnam, or Watergate, he replied, "I am a New Testament evangelist, not an Old Testament prophet." Behind that response lies the story that we convert individuals and individuals convert society. Certainly change would not occur if persons did not see the need for it, but a changed person in an unchanged system usually does not make much difference. Those evangelicals who aspire to get their kind of Christian in high places fail to understand the limited impact individuals can have when the systems do not correspond to their values. A cadre of Christian presidents in corporations will not make a sufficient difference to those getting hurt unless there is a corresponding revision of the economic order. Freedom of the self within the bondage of the system is good but not sufficient. The bondage must be unwound. Liberation theology draws into focus the need to transform structures as a way of enabling freedom to emerge. Economic analysis reveals the degree to which those structures prevent freedom even for liberated people; and it can propose alternate structures which help to begin and sustain the journey toward freedom.

Even if we have resolved the issue of where to begin, something else comes into play. Our lives are always at the center of several types of stories, each competing for allegiance. There are those which assure the present will prevail and lend their weight to its permanence; they engender futurelessness and intercept the journey toward freedom. American civil religion calls us to honor and respect but never to challenge the nation. Our economic order is dominated by large corporations whose growth and survival is fostered by stability. Both civil religion and the economic system provide stories that elevate and canonize the present. However, there are other stories that break open the present to allow a new future to develop; they enable the journey toward freedom by desacralizing the existing power structures. These are the biblical stories—and they are another story altogether. The resurrection is paradigmatic. One of its meanings is that God pries open the future at the very moment humankind seems most surely to have shut it down. Easter day is the story of a future breaking open the present rather than growing out of the present. There is a demand for the present to become what it was meant to be. "What ought to be" overpowers "what is." That story—and others that foreshadow and fulfill it—are kept alive in a storytelling fellowship. The people of God tell the stories of God and live them out until the journey toward freedom takes hold. The priority of the future replaces the stories that have upheld the prevailing order.

Above all, the reality of God in the stories makes the difference. That content in the stories is in large measure a funcion of where we are when we speak of God. If we are posted in our existential needs, grounded in philosophical analysis, or vexed by the mysteries and processes of nature, that will fashion our understanding of God. Liberation theology need not repudiate those vantage points in order to set the priority of another. Consistent with its plea for a theology from below, our words about God must be spoken from within the bondage created by oppression and the suffering engendered by systems and institutions that dehumanize. Academic theology comes only after we have listened to and worked with the black youth unable to find employment, the worker who has no power to assert human rights when a recession threatens, or the older person abandoned by family, friends, and society. Nothing is more crucial in setting the agenda for our lives and for the principalities and powers than the realization that the "Lord works vindication and justice for all who are oppressed" (Psalms 103:6). To speak of God as in solidarity with those who are getting hurt in our world forces us to face tasks previously unimagined and makes relentless demands upon us and our society.

Economists, of course, do not speak of God. The deity does not fit on graphs, nor does "the holy one" enter into analytic schemes. Tied down by the analytic structure, economists too often opt for gradualism, which in reality becomes accommodation to the prevailing order and en-

sures maintenance of the status quo. But economics becomes "another story" when what God is doing in the world
for human freedom and fulfillment weighs in as a controlling
feature. That does awesome things to one's agenda. Assumptions long embraced are scrutinized, and dispassion-
ate analysis is shown to be insufficient. When the poor and
the oppressed are seen as a "mask of God," radical change
may become an imperative rather than an intellectual game.
For an economist to have on his conscience a suffering God
renders issues of human choice in the system, the exploitive nature of production mechanisms, and the distribution
of resources in relation to human need into a form where
crucifixion and resurrection are dominant metaphors. Then
one is drawn to search for solutions that allow accumulated
wealth and bureaucratic power to serve the needs of all in
the society and not just the needs of a few.

The question remains of how one is to carry out the new
agenda. The predominant stories in our culture assign to
religion the task of elevating contemplation over action,
submission over subversion, reformation over revolution,
and reconciliation over liberation. While a few stories seek
to invert the order, the prevailing plot is one that either
preserves present arrangements or enables rather painless
alterations over time. Underneath those stories is the
"America, love it or leave it" mentality. What is unique in
the biblical story is that it holds both poles in view. It re-
fuses on ideological grounds to baptize the options on one
side and villainize those on the other. Each pole is always a
possibility; the strength of the device is in having to work
through the validity of each. Often one finds that the alternatives complement and strengthen each other. Liberation
and reconciliation, for example, do not always preclude
each other and fall into a given sequence. Aspects of each
overlap at times and in their collision move the world in
ways that neither could without the other. To live in biblical
stories where the "God of hope" is centered is to accept as
one's own the journey toward freedom and not be bound by
the road maps of those whose ideologies constrain the future.

The Journey toward Freedom

1 Enlarging the Liberation Agenda

Theologians often fail to acknowledge positively the degree to which theology depends upon mood. The word does not necessarily mean an arbitrary emotional disposition. Indeed, mood is a "pervasive temper of mind": it denotes the "mental disposition" that lies beneath the ways in which our thought and experience are ordered.[1] The word is bound to feelings but feelings have correlates in thought. With theology much conceptual work rides on moods within the culture or a particular society. Some dismiss that as faddish; much of it may be. Paul Tillich did not write of moods, but he affirmed "situation" as one pole of the theological effort. He meant by that "the scientific and artistic, the economic, political, and ethical forms" in which the nature of existence is interpreted. For Tillich, "situation" is much more than "mood," but when he refers to "all kinds of psychological and sociological conditions" it is evident that he means not less than moods.[2] One might even contend that the full range of factors he mentions as giving shape and form to our situation in some degree rides on moods.

It hardly needs to be argued that contemporary theology has been marked by excessive variety and vacillation. In contrast to former times in which terms like *liberalism* and *neoorthodoxy* covered an era, no one brand of theology controls or orchestrates the enterprise now. Neither coherence nor comprehensiveness is a characteristic of the scene. The theoscape is marked by rapid and often erratic shifts. What informs and fashions our work is what theologians, wittingly or not, detect to be the mood, sometimes of

19

the hour. The modal terms even emerge at times in the discourse of the professionals—despair, cynicism, festivity, optimism. Moods in our time appear to shift rapidly, often without warning and without apparent reason. Their passion of late appears to have intensified and occasioned the variety and vacillation. That need not be written off as evidence of faddishness. To be free of moods would be to attempt irrigation from dry springs. Theology is fed from moods, though not defined by them.

The present mood in our society is a difficult one for those who have a commitment to see liberation as the theme that enables us to penetrate and articulate the biblical message. The flower children have been de-flowered, and their loss of innocence leaves optimism without a psychic center of support. The passion for justice and the outrage at injustice has been drained off by quests for mystical encounter and journeys into self-actualization. The confidence in right triumphing over wrong that energizes social change has receded, leaving bare a mind set where contentment is the goal. Empathy with suffering and "the wretched of the earth" has been replaced by apathy in the face of the future and opportunism in the present. A theology built in an era erupting in activism has now to compete in an era in which stasis is honored. How does one pursue liberation theology when the current mood undermines the tension between "what is" and "what ought to be"?

A. Liberation Theology and Storytelling

For every generation the task of theology has been to construct a version of the Christian faith responsive to the imbeddedness of God in human affairs. In biblical texts God's name appears most commonly in relation to events. The theologian's task is to identify events in the present that resemble those to which God's name has previously been linked. Making sense of the incarnation for one's own time is the axial point. Liberation theology in our era centers on the journey toward freedom as the fundamental human drama occasioned by what God is doing in history. The liberation theologian sees the issue of freedom lodged in the structural similarity between oppression in biblical times and in our own. It is not surprising that blacks, feminists, and Third World nations have been the most responsive to the issue of liberation. Most liberation theologians in America have been slow to realize that we live and write vicariously, without any clear recognition that we are not the oppressed. Theology that emerges from another's experience cannot long be meaningful. If liberation theology is to be viable for those of us who are neither blacks, nor feminists, nor Third World citizens, the base of experience will have to be enlarged to include us. It may be important to recognize that we enter as the oppressors, but that is not sufficient. If liberation is to be a theme that engages our being, it must relate to more than our negative behaviors and the borrowed experiences of others.

One anecdotal example of the narrowness of liberation theology is the response of a college freshman who had been especially grasped by James Cone's *A Black Theology of Liberation*. He was ready to sign up as a disciple—on the basis of borrowed experience—but then his own experience interceded. His father died. The young man said later, "James Cone meant nothing to me when I had to cope with death." Cone's theology was not written to that experience, and the student's expectations were unfair. No black academic has a specific responsibility to help an upper-class white come to terms with the realities of life. Yet there is a point which ought not to be lost: if liberation theology is singularly fixed to systemic oppression, it may not embrace the existential anguish in human experience. We need an understanding of freedom that is fundamental to the full range of human experiences.

The reconstruction of liberation theology can begin with the recognition that "the formal quality of experience through time is inherently narrative."[3] Storytelling has inordinate power and persuasiveness for putting persons in touch with the reality of their existence. As Harvey Cox writes, "through our stories we assemble our pasts, place ourselves in the present, and cast a hope for the future. Without stories we would be bereft of memory and anticipation."[4] Stories often provide the integrating structure through which we understand. Our consciousness is molded by narratives; for many, they are the substance for thought about ourselves and human existence. Stories extend our range of consciousness and increase the density of existence. The most important parts of oneself can only be identified and communicated to oneself and others by storytelling. One can say, for example, that one's father died at a given time when one was a certain age. That is fact. But when we want to possess the event and uncover what it meant, we have to begin a process of storytelling—who told us and how we reacted, what we did the next day, the experience of riding in the hearse, how friends treated us, what it was like to forget one's father was dead. All of those factors and many others have to come forward in story form. They and they alone are adequate to put us and others in touch with the reality. There is very little of consequence that can be said without recourse to narrative. We live in and through stories—our own and those of others.

By contrast, "the inability to tell a story leaves an unintelligible residue in our lives that is too large."[5] There is a loss of identity and self-understanding that diminishes and victimizes us. Our feelings are never collected and ordered, and our sense of self contracts in the measure we forget or avoid our stories. To be without a story is to sink into a present we do not understand, to be manipulated by a past over which we have no control, and to be the victims of a capricious future whose mercy is at best uncertain. Our "passage" becomes one in which we do not know who we are or what we are about. To disenfranchise our personal stories is to cut off our access to the reality of our existence and narrow our experience to a series of unexamined feelings. Largeness of being recedes. Implicit in the argument of future chapters is the assumption that those who have no story of their own are especially vulnerable to the stories imposed on them by the institutions of society.

But stories of ourselves are not the only narratives in which we may live and identify ourselves. "Our personal stories are often made conscious because of an archetypal story at the foundations of consciousness."[6] That is, our culture has stories similar to our own which evoke not only awareness of ourselves but also larger narratives within which our "incidents" find their place. In the eighty-first year of his life, psychologist C. G. Jung began to dictate "the story of his inner life." He wrestled with the question of his story and the one in which it fit. On the larger scale he asked himself, "But in what myth does man live nowadays? In the Christian Myth the answer might be, 'Do you live in it?' I ask myself. To be honest, the answer was no. For me, it is not what I live by . . . 'but then what is your myth—the myth in which you do live?' "[7] Jung was acknowledging that he and every person functions within a story, lives in a myth. No life is free of a plot, a larger conception of things that gives coherence, provides meaning, and exerts control. Whether or not we are able to articulate it carefully and consciously, we function on its terms.

An authentic articulation of the biblical faith has the character of a story. The message lends itself to narrative and requires it as a form. In one sense there is very little theology in the Old and New Testaments, but there is an abundance of narrative. Biblical writers were not given to abstraction and speculation; concreteness and particularity are the characteristics of their language. The birth of Christ is told three times in story form in the synoptic gospels. Because they exist, the Gospel of John, for instance, can give a philosophical account of the Word becoming flesh. It is significant that the most common form of teaching in the ministry of Jesus was the parable. The heart of his message was the kingdom of God. There is very little if anything said about the kingdom in propositional form. Typically, Jesus began, "The kingdom of God is like . . ." Then there followed a story or metaphor. The New Testament has the Old as precedent. There, biblical writers told the stories of origin, destiny, deviation, and fulfillment. The book of Genesis is one story layered on another.

Thus there is a correlation and comparability between our need for a story that gives context and for stories that enable us to tell our story in ways we had not before. Stories are the media by which we move both within ourselves toward our depths and beyond ourselves toward a horizon and a framework unconditioned by our finitude. Stories struggle to put us in touch with our reality, and reality moves toward us in story form. God and humankind both love stories. We need them.

What may be of particular importance in liberation theology is the power of stories to create experience. Stories can do more than capture our experience and name it for us. They have the capacity to put us in touch with phenomena in human history that we have lost. Stories give us access to experiences we would otherwise be denied. Jewish novelist Elie Wiesel retells the story of four generations of rabbis.[8] When facing misfortune with his people, the first rabbi went to a special place in the forest, lit a fire, and said a prayer, and misfortune was averted. A generation later his successor went to the same place in the forest and said, "Master of the universe, listen! I do not know how to light the fire but I am still able to say the prayer." There began the retreat from religious experience, but the misfortune was averted. The third generation rabbi went into the forest and said, "I do not know how to light the fire, I do not know the prayer, but I know the place and this must be sufficient." And it was. Now when misfortune came again, the fourth rabbi said, sitting in his armchair, "I am unable to light the fire and I do not know the prayer; I cannot even find the place in the forest. All I can do is to tell the story and this must be sufficient." And telling the story had the same effect as the actions of the other three. Stories can do for us what we cannot do for ourselves: re-create or sustain our relation to things that otherwise would elude us.

Biblical stories tell the story of liberation, "the actualization of freedom,"[9] and they have the power to create the dynamics and sensibility of freedom in the absence of both. They can activate the "wish to be free."

But the problem may be that many versions of the Christian faith are short stories. They are complete within themselves, but their scope is narrow and limited. They relate to one facet of experience and not our human experience in its complexity. That may indeed be the limitation of many versions of liberation theology. In their determination to address the circumstance of oppression in its social, political, and economic forms there is a failure to tell a story with enough wholeness. What we need is a story that is prismatic with respect to our experience and through which our thinking is transfigured. It is through story that "experience has changed a way of thinking, and a way of thinking has changed experience."[10] The plot must engage all the elements of our experience of ourselves.

B. Freeing Liberation

The agenda for liberation theology, then, has as a priority enlarging the term *liberation*. There is no justification for weakening its adhesions to the conditions under which our freedom is impaired. Political, social, and economic systems and institutions restrict severely what Paul Lehmann refers to as the time and space to be human. Oppression of blacks, women, and Third World citizens is not addressed by the restitution of interpersonal niceties. Sexist roles are not affected by helping your wife with the dishes; racist structures are not overcome by being decent to your black laundress; malnutrition is not addressed by the proverbial turkey basket prepared by the senior high fellowship; Third World colonialism is not rectified by exchange students. Freedom is at the mercy of the social ecology. The environment in the fullest sense defines the terms within which we function and actualize ourselves. Liberation theology necessarily and inevitably addresses the issue of human context.

Without diminishing its concern with structures and institutions, liberation theology needs to address the issue of freedom in all the forms that confront and contort the human species. We need to address the death in racism without ignoring the death of that student's father and the human anguish it represents. We need a story that tells the whole story. While that is more than anyone can deliver, it deserves to preside over our aspirations. Perhaps the concept of liberation will begin to spread if we talk about it as centering on the actualization of freedom. Becoming free is a process of living *in*, living *above*, and living *against* one's circumstances. It occurs whenever there is a break in the condition of futurelessness, in which the shutdown on openness to possibilities is overcome. The occasion for freedom is understood biblically not as emerging from human initiatives or systemic self-alterations. "It is rather the insertion of a new reality into history in such a way that the closed present is broken open for the new."[11] Freedom has its origin in the incursions of God. The biblical story is a narrative laying out God's initiatives for freedom.

In order to get a sense of this we need to attend to some narratives and themes. As a prelude, it is important to explore briefly the phenomenon of praxis. Liberation theologians of all brands advance it as a primary method for biblical appropriation. Praxis precludes beginning with abstractions and overlaying them on experience; it is grounded in concreteness and particularity. Theology emerges *"after the fact"* as Christians "reflect about facts and experiences which have already evoked a response from Christians."[12] Reflection follows action in which the faithful are involved. Far from being an advance game plan, theology becomes an endeavor to state the faith as an account of the action of the faithful. The theology of liberation emerges slowly from within concrete and particular experiences. It is not a systematic theology concerned with arranging "all discoveries or conclusions into one overarching system."[13] Given the convergence of action and reflections, a more fluid state becomes normal. When everything settles down into place—orderly, neat, and precise—praxis is no longer operative and theological calcification has occurred. Movements within the concreteness and particularity of historical existence keep theologians with an aspiration for a stable system off balance. The questions get revised, the circumstances modified, the observations change and the reflection and formulation that follow have flux as a steady component. In the course of these changes, the nature of truth itself is transformed. Some even go as far as to say that "action is itself the truth. Truth is at the level of history, not in the realm of ideas. Reflection on praxis, on human significant action, can only be authentic when it is done from within, in the vicinity of the strategic and tactical plane of human action."[14]

While liberation theology begins in the responsiveness of Christians to events and collates that with biblical narratives, it is not often made clear that praxis itself is biblical. That is, biblical writers did not begin with ideas or doctrines but with concrete and particular events in which Israelites and Christians were involved. Obviously, the biblical material is not itself theology in any formal or academic sense. The fact remains that we have these narratives because persons reflected upon the action in which they were participants or observers. The Exodus narratives were not written ahead of history or on the basis of theological postulates. The people of Israel were engaged in a struggle for freedom in which they came to believe God was a covenant partner. Action and reflection converged to develop the notion of God as deliverer or liberator from their bondage. The faith claims that emerged were grounded in the experience of a faithful community. In a sense the blueprint is devised concurrently with the event and the time that follows. Thus we look to these events to relive them, not to stylize conclusions. As we penetrate their concreteness and particularity we may find them corresponding in remarkable ways to our own. Our task is to look back and forth between the action/reflection of former times and our action/reflection in the radicality of this time. The structural similarity should enable us to live in, live above, and live against the full range of human circumstances. Biblical folk never accept immersion in their private and public conditions, and we need to understand the origin of their buoyancy. Paul Lehmann writing on Karl Barth names him a "theologian of permanent revolution."[15] Lehmann focuses on aspects of Barth's theology—and the biblical witness— that forbid ideological discipleship, accommodation to worldly pressures, and a prone acceptance of existence as given. Permanent revolution means that the people of God are always living in, living above, and living against their personal and public circumstances. An essential homelessness prevails; a dialectic of place and destiny controls the experience of existence. To exist authentically is to be on the way, never having arrived. Every disposition to nest in a condition, a system, a task, or a place is overcome by a process of divestiture. Biblical folk move on; they are uprooted.

C. Two Stories: Liberation and Our Consciousness

There are some stories in the Old and New Testaments that point us to the larger story, the story of liberation as the actualization of freedom, of persons living in, living above, and living against their circumstances. That story, in course, will become agenda setting for both the economist and the theologian. Exposition may reveal the texture of existence when it is biblically informed.

Abram and Sara laughed at God. A promise had been given to Abram: from his loins would emerge a unique people who would be a blessing to humankind. In years to come he would be known by the Israelites as "Abraham, our Father." But Sara was barren—how could one become the father of a nation without children? The custom of the day gave them one option. Sara offered her servant, Hagar, to her husband and from that a son was born whom they called Ishmael. Abram then told God the promise was on the way to fulfillment.

God may have appreciated their resourcefulness, but it was not "the intended fulfillment." In their next conversation, Abram found his name changed to Abraham. Names have significance in the Old Testament because they convey meanings about the person. Abraham means "father of many." The message was clear: Abraham and Sara would have a child. At the moment one might have expected rejoicing, the two of them laughed in the face of God, for Abraham was ninety-nine and Sara ninety—not prime time for a pregnancy. After they recovered from the spell of laughter, Abraham sought to ease God's embarrassment—obviously he had lost touch with the cycles of nature. The proposal was that Ishmael be counted as making good on the promise. But God said, "No, Sara your wife will bear a son."

When the child came they named him Isaac. And Sara said, "God has made laughter for me; everyone who hears will laugh over me!" The Hebrew word for laughter is *Isaac*. This old man and this old woman who began laughing at God named the fulfillment of their dreams "laughter."

In the narrative laughter was a means of passage into an open future. An open future is one free of the constraints that make persons narrow and small. Possibilities have free reign; life opens up rather than closes in. Existential anguish is bypassed. Laughter becomes an agent of liberation, of persons living in, living above, and living against their circumstances.

Sara and Abraham were trapped "in the cold logic of human reason, with its time charts and rhythmic opportunities for pregnancy."[16] They thought it realistic at the ages of ninety-nine and ninety to settle for Ishmael. But the issue was not biology; it was the authority of the present. Abraham had been given a promise; he would be the "father of many." Even knowing the credentials of him who made the promise, Abraham elected to live within present reality.

The issue was whether to live by promise or by prediction. If by prediction, reason and charts hold full sway. Fate's definition of the future would prevail. If by promise, then they would live by wild and risky expectation. Abraham and Sara had to decide whether to live in terms of what had come forth or what was forthcoming. It was laughter that in large measure facilitated the transition from prediction to promise. The comic occurred in the moment of disparity. The promise of a son conflicted with the hard realities of nature. They laughed when God restated the promise, but the laughter enabled them to double-cross themselves, to subvert "the cold logic of human reason." It made relative what was presented and accepted as reality. The future began to open; laughter was the bridge between the persuasion of prediction and the whimsicalness of promise.

Perhaps the better way to say it is that laughter is the means by which hope is restored. Clearly, Sara and Abraham had drawn in their horizon. They accommodated their expectations to what lay at hand. Ishmael was good enough as a fulfillment of God's promises. But God stood with those promises, and in the moment they laughed at their prospects, those promises began to take hold. It put them in touch with the "not yet," in their lives. "Laughter is hope's last weapon. . . . It shows that despite the disappearance of an empirical basis for hope, we have not stopped hoping."[17]

Through laughter, Abraham and Sara participated in the actualization of freedom, the appropriation of a future they had no right to expect. They lived for a time in the laughter of God. In their laughter "a sense of wild, irrational hope"[18] was freed to transform their consciousness. In living by promises they were changed as persons.

D. Two Stories: Liberation and the Present Order

Jesus had been carefully maneuvering his disciples into a position where they might understand who he was and what he was about. Most recently he had been in dialogue with Peter: "Whom do men say that I am?" he inquired of the impetuous disciple. Peter replied, "You are the Christ, the son of the living God." On the heels of that discussion, Jesus took Peter, and the brothers James and John, up a high mountain. There the three had an astonishing experience—their hero was transfigured, a metamorphosis occurred. "His face shone like the sun; his garments became white as light" (Matthew 17:2). He was wrapped in a glory they had not seen before, and he was believed to be in conversation with Elijah and Moses. Peter's response was the strongest; it was an incredible experience and he wanted to prolong it: "Let me build three booths, one for you, and one for Moses, and one for Elijah." But then "a bright cloud overshadowed them." In biblical times, clouds were associated with the presence of God. They were the mask from behind which God spoke. A voice said, "This is my beloved Son, with whom I am well pleased; listen to Him." The disciples were "filled with awe" and prostrated themselves on the ground. In the midst of an ecstasy they could neither grasp nor control, Jesus "touched them." The one who had been removed from the ordinary, transfigured beyond anything their imagination could anticipate, performed the most human gesture—he "touched them." When they looked up, only Jesus was there.

The story intensified the disciples' awareness that they were living in a moment of overlap; it was a time when one age was struggling to be born while another appeared to be in control. A tension was felt between "what is" and "what ought to be." "What is going on is the pressure of the end-time upon time rapidly coming to an end."[19] The new age is pushing the present order beyond its limits. When the disciples saw Jesus, they knew time was running out on this world, God was "breaking in and breaking up"[20] the powers and structures that prevailed. An inescapable and inevitable present was met head on by the assurance of its defeat. All that appeared secure had its vulnerability revealed. The beginning of the end for the old order was bringing about the end of the beginning for the new one. The transfiguration signals a countdown on whose world this is and whose will is to prevail.[21] The new age seems powerless to be born, yet a benediction has been passed over the old, ending its claim to a finality beyond its reach. Through the transfiguration the disciples were opened to a "messianic secret": there is immanent in our world a God who pierces the configurations of power that keep the present what it is. God breaks in and breaks up, enabling the faithful to live in, live above, and live against present circumstances.

Every decision the disciples made from that point on was a vote for one age or another, for things as they are or things as they are intended to be. The transfiguration meant that what seemed so powerful was perishing and what seemed so powerless was poised for enactment. They could line up with the breaking in and breaking up or with the holding fast and staying put. They could align themselves with the journey toward freedom or with the configurations of oppression. They could be part of an establishment organized to protect itself against the age to be or become part of the incursion by a humanly desirable future. The choice was between one order mighty in its death throes and another weak in its birth pains.

The transfiguration means that God has made the actualization of freedom in time *and* space a possibility. The present order is desacralized. The power of its structures no longer prevails.

Two stories do not tell the whole story, but they tell enough of the story to communicate that living in, living above, and living against is essential to the biblical narrative. They may draw us into the process of not only telling our own story but beginning as well our own journey toward freedom. "Storytelling is a movement toward an unconditional horizon. On the way toward an archetypal story we learn to tell our personal story. Possibility is conjoined with actuality to reveal the reality of our own becoming."[22] The archetypal stories can pull us beyond ourselves and precipitate the movement toward liberation in our private and in our corporate lives.

The story of Sara and Abraham carries the promise of changing persons; the story of the transfiguration carries the promise of changing the power structures of society. In the following chapters, the interplay, dominance, and ambience of these two stories will protrude from time to time. Imbedded in both economic structures and theological perspectives will be stories that either assume or prescribe the priority of impacting human consciousness or transforming the order of society.

Notes

1. *Webster's New International Dictionary of the English Language* (Springfield, Mass.: G. & C. Merriam Co., 1955), s.v. "mood."
2. Paul Tillich, *Systematic Theology,* 3 vols. (Chicago: University of Chicago Press, 1951), 1: 3–4.
3. Stephen Crites, "The Narrative Quality of Experience," *Journal of American Academy of Religion* (1971), p. 271.
4. Harvey Cox, *The Seduction of the Spirit* (New York: Simon and Schuster, 1973), p. 12.
5. Charles E. Winquest, "The Act of Storytelling and of the Self's Homecoming," *Journal of American Academy of Religion* 42, no. 1 (March 1974): 103.
6. Ibid., p. 109.
7. C. G. Jung, *Memories, Dreams, Reflections* (New York: Vintage Books, 1963), p. 171.
8. Elie Wiesel, *The Gates of the Forest* (New York: Holt, Rinehart and Winston, 1966), pp. 82–83.
9. Peter C. Hodgson, *New Birth of Freedom: A Theology of Bondage and Liberation* (Philadelphia: Fortress Press, 1976), pp. 265ff.
10. Paul Lehmann, *The Transfiguration of Politics* (New York: Harper and Row, 1975), p. 24.
11. Rubem Alves, *A Theology of Human Hope* (Washington/Cleveland: Corpus Books, 1969), p. 105.
12. José Miguez Bonino, *Doing Theology in a Revolutionary Situation* (Philadelphia: Fortress Press, 1975), p. 61.
13. Letty M. Russell, *Human Liberation in Feminist Perspective: A Theology* (Philadelphia: Westminster Press, 1974), p. 55.
14. Bonino, *Doing Theology,* p. 72.

15. Paul Lehmann, *Union Seminary Quarterly Review* 28, no. 1 (1972): 67–81.
16. Joseph C. McLelland, *The Clown and the Crocodile* (Richmond, Va.: John Knox Press, 1970), p. 27.
17. Harvey Cox, *Feast of Fools* (Cambridge, Mass.: Harvard Univ. Press, 1969), p. 157.
18. Peter Berger, *The Precarious Vision* (Garden City, N.Y.: Doubleday, 1961), p. 213.
19. Paul Lehmann, *The Transfiguration of Politics*, p. 80.
20. Ibid., p. 80.
21. Ibid., p. 83.
22. Winquest, "The Act of Storytelling," pp. 112–13.

2   Stories, Institutions, and Economics

The use of story is alien to the analytic economist. Educated in the tradition of Smith, Mill, Marshall, Keynes, and Samuelson, most modern economists interpret events and behavior by applying their analytic tools and examining quantitative data. Economists think of themselves as living by cold reason and logic, not by stories; but they often ignore the wide range of assumptions and assertions that are carried in their analytic structure. Economists rarely question the utilitarianism of Jeremy Bentham or the profit maximization of any modern textbook. Such assumptions and assertions are value laden in the sense that they express the way things ought to be. For example, when we assume that a producer will act to maximize profit, we are tacitly contending that the society values such behavior highly. However, profit maximization is not a basic human desire; it is a culturally based value. There are two questions we might raise about these assumptions: Does the society really value such behavior? and, Should the society value such behavior? These are agenda-setting questions that the analytic economist almost never asks.

There are economists who are willing to challenge the existing sets of assumptions and to interpret events and behavior differently. At the beginning of the twentieth century, Thorstein Veblen was developing the tenets of institutional economics. He argued that the analytic structure of economics grew out of and was peculiar to that set of institutional structures which happened to dominate a society at a given time. Economic analysis is actually the beginning of a story that attempts to interpret reality; as such, the theory is neither timeless nor universal. Despite all pretensions to being scientific and value free, the heart of modern economic theory lies not with its analytic structure and its elaborate box of tools but with its unspoken assumptions and value premises. John Kenneth Galbraith also challenges the pretensions of analytic economists. He goes further than Veblen when he claims that many of the economic institutions currently existing in the United States cannot be interpreted in terms of the analytic structure and the associated assumptions of economists. Not only is the economists' methodology based on a series of unspoken assumptions, but the assumptions are defective.

Most economists have been trapped by their methodology. They do not know how to include value premises explicitly in their analyses, so they ignore them. The analytic structures resist modification and must be abandoned when societal values change. If a society begins to value human need over profit, the economists' tools cannot cope with the change. The tools are tuned to respond to signals that no longer exist. Another part of the problem is that values are not quantitative; they cannot be measured. In addition, economists are trained to ignore values, not to interpret them. If economists are to have an active role in societal change then they must begin to address values questions. Before including such questions within economic analysis, it is necessary to decide which values, how they are transmitted, and the means by which they are changed. Stories are a central way in which values are transmitted and receptivity to them is created.

In chapter 1 the transfiguration narrative was interpreted as a clash between the old order and a new one. The old one supported and was supported by a set of values that included the desire for stability and the maintenance of the existing arrangements. The new order was to be formed by a different vision of "what ought to be." While the odds overwhelmingly favored "what is," the transfiguration story points to something more powerful than the present. The power of God is at large. As the story is told and retold, the vision of "what ought to be" creates a new set of values and reinforces them. Human freedom and fulfillment become more important than stability and power. In the face of an all-powerful existing order, the story plays a role in establishing a new set of values and aligning people with the enactment of a new order. Can stories also be a medium by which old and new economic values are developed, passed on, and changed?

A. Stories and Economic Values

David McClelland has substantiated an economic role for stories in *The Achieving Society*. In a series of experiments he demonstrated that stories are a primary means by which cultural groups and nations articulate economic values and pass them on to succeeding generations. A range of economic values was expressed in stories drawn from the cultures McClelland examined. He discovered a high degree of correlation between particular values and the observed economic success of the cultures from which they emerged. Greater economic rewards consistently accrued in those societies whose stories featured economic achievement.

McClelland was interested in the causes of economic development. He argued that economic growth is more likely to occur if the culture values achievement.[1] The existence of an achievement motive was demonstrated in the following experiment. Two randomly selected groups of students were tested. The first group took two tests. As a prelude to test 1 they were told that this particular test would indicate intelligence, administrative capacity, ability to organize material, potential for evaluating crucial situations quickly and accurately, and suitability for leadership. The test instructions were designed to arouse an achievement motivation if one existed. Both groups took test 2, which was a series of pictures flashed on a screen for a few seconds. "The pictures represented a variety of life situations centering particularly around work."[2] In response, each participant was asked to fantasize and write a story. The first group took test 2 immediately after having any potential achievement motivations aroused by the conditions of test 1. The second group took only test 2, with no achievement-motivation-arousing conditions. Thus any broad differences that occurred in the fantasy stories for the two groups can be traced to the arousal of achievement motive in the first group.

When the stories written by the two groups were compared, "differences immediately became apparent. The stories written under 'aroused' conditions contained more references to 'standards of excellence' and to doing well, or wanting to do well, with respect to the standards."[3] These results indicate that an achievement motive does exist; achievement orientations in personal fantasy were evoked by the test conditions imposed upon the first group. Further tests have indicated that the existence of a potential achievement motive is not limited to economically advanced cultures. The initial experiment was conducted with groups of male American college students. Similar results, however, have been obtained with experiments involving Navaho Indians and Brazilian students.[4]

The next problem lies in measuring the strength of the achievement motive. McClelland used ambiguous pictures to evoke fantasy responses. Therefore, if an individual who has not been subject to "achievement arousal" consistently uses achievement related ideas in stories, there is "a strong 'inner concern' with achievement."[5] From this McClelland derives a very simple measure of achievement motivation. He counts the instances of achievement-related ideas in stories written without the achievement-arousal stimulus. He calls this measure "n achievement."

Many research projects have examined the behaviors of individual subjects with high and low n achievement scores. They show that high n achievement scores among American males tend to be associated with the middle class, with persons who are active in organizations and communities, with resistance to social pressure, and with a desire to work with others who have expertise.[6] High *n* achievers tend to perform significantly better in complex tasks where the emphasis is on doing the job well. Finally, they are motivated internally to set their own standards and to achieve them. McClelland's test results indicate that *n* achievement exists, that it can be measured, and that its consequences include a high degree of self-motivation with a drive to succeed. It is virtually impossible to use the same test procedures to isolate and measure the existence of an achievement motive for whole societies. However, McClelland needed such a broad societal measure if he was to relate the achievement motive to economic growth and development.

Like Weber and Tawney before him, McClelland points out that the values associated with the Protestant work ethic could lead to a higher level of *n* achievement in countries that were predominantly Protestant. This in turn should lead to a more rapid pace of economic development and a higher level of economic achievement. At least for countries in temperate climates, the evidence he presents supports this hypothesis.[7] This association of religious background and affiliation with achievement motivations is, however, too simplistic and too general. There is clearly a variety of social and cultural influences that contribute to high achievement motivation and its corollary, high achievement. McClelland wanted to find some measure that would indicate when these influences should be present and when not. The hypothesis was that if such influences existed, they would be transmitted from generation to generation. The transmission process would spread the values. When *n* achievement exists in a society, some of the values being transmitted relate to success motivation, individual self-expression, achievement, and reward.

The experimenters isolated the existence of *n* achievement in both past and present societies by examining two types of stories: folk tales in preliterate societies, and written children's stories in literate societies. The same measure of *n* achievement was used for both: a count of the average number of achievement related ideas in each story for each culture. For the preliterate cultures, a collection of twelve stories from each of fifty different cultures was used as the data base. The stories were similar; the same subjects were treated in each culture; the manner of telling and the structure of the stories were different. The stories were coded for n achievement levels and then correlated with several variables that might indicate possibilities for growth and development. Existence of significant entrepreneurial activity was much more strongly present in the high n achievement cultures.[8] One conclusion to be drawn from this is that cultures that value individual achievement and entrepreneurial activity seem to have developed folk stories that focus on achievement. These stories are one mechanism for passing on these values to the next generation.

A similar but even more dramatic result appears when the written children's stories are analyzed. McClelland included virtually all of the countries of Europe, North America, and Oceania as well as some in Latin America and Asia. He found that those countries whose children's stories scored high in n achievement tended to be countries that were also overachievers in terms of several measures of economic change and growth. In fact, n achievement levels acted as a significant predictor of economic growth between 1925 and 1950 and again in the post-1950 period.[9] The conclusion is that the stories that gained wide currency within those countries were descriptive of societal values that favor and foster economic growth. Clearly, countries like the United States that have succeeded in economic terms have strong systems of reward for individual accomplishment and a value system that rates economic success very highly. McClelland is contending that the stories we have always used to help our children learn how to read and communicate can carry the additional impact of transmitting ideas and values favorable to the formation of self-motivation, individual initiative, and entrepreneurial activity. Such values reinforce the economic growth ethic and foster a stronger success motivation in each new generation.

McClelland's experiments make it clear that for individuals economic values can indeed be formed, transmitted, and even changed through the medium of stories. If the story of Sara and Abraham with its focus on transformation of consciousness is sufficient, then McClelland's analysis would argue that building a better society requires only the formulation of new personal stories.

B. Institutional Formation

The emphasis on changing individuals is inadequate; the values created and passed on through the dominance of certain stories cannot be fully felt and carried out unless supportive institutional structures emerge. Any society accomplishes much of its normal activity because institutional arrangements automate the day-to-day decision making. These institutions are effective in decision making because they create a predictable and at least tacitly acceptable pattern of relationships between individuals, groups, and institutions themselves. We do not need continually to make personal decisions to obey laws, pay taxes, or go to work each day. The structures of society tend to make such decisions for us without our giving them regular conscious thought. We do not need to concern ourselves with making goods and services available. The institution of the market provides them, and we normally are concerned only with consumer choices.

Such institutions evolve slowly. The process begins when an attitude or an idea emerges. At first held by a handful of people, and probably passed on in story form, such ideas are often in contradiction with generally held beliefs. Slowly the idea begins to gain more credence and wider acceptance and takes on the character of a "value." It becomes identified as what ought to be. In order for this new value to survive, it needs some structures to reinforce it and to ensure its being passed on. This is the stage at which institutions need to be developed, or the value may be lost.

Institutions emerge in response to changing values and,

paradoxically, in an effort to maintain values in the face of change. As the values are accepted, the institutions that support them become stronger and more powerful. When values begin to change, when newer ideas and attitudes begin to be felt, or when other stories begin to be told, the existing order resists the change. The institutional structures that support the existing values have attained a good deal of economic or political power or social status. It is difficult for those institutions to give up their power and status in the face of new values that call for other structures. The old institutions become obstacles to any further change in the structure of the society and inhibit or even prevent the spread of the new values.

An example drawn from European history may help to focus the critical issues involved in institutional formation and perpetuation. After the fall of the Roman Empire, chaotic political conditions led to extensive instability and insecurity throughout much of western Europe. The absence of institutions capable of providing law and order left the weak at the mercy of the strong. The need for personal security became one of the dominant values in the society. Ultimately, the weak chose to relinquish some of their personal freedom in exchange for the protection afforded by their stronger neighbors. This choice included giving up the rights to their land and its products, an act which bought the weak a measure of protection but enhanced the power of those who were already strong. Thus the institution of feudalism was established and gathered strength. It developed as an intricate interweaving of rights and responsibilities between the serf and the feudal lord. As long as the need for security and protection was strongly felt, the power of the feudal lords and of the institution of feudalism itself was enhanced.

Eventually, the power of the interlocking web of feudal lords and of feudalistic rights became entrenched. It grew out of all proportion to the protection or security provided to the serfs and others who had ostensibly given up their lands and their freedom for those benefits. As cities and kings became more powerful and as new values of nationalism and individualism began to emerge in western Europe, the feudalistic institutions were dismantled. There was, however, a long period of struggle as the feudal lords fought to hold on to the power, status, and perquisites they had gained. The institutions reacted to survive and to prevent the new values from emerging. The stories that dominated societies at that time focused on the glories of the feudalistic state. They helped to maintain feudalism in the face of changing societal needs.

Veblen argued that such institutions eventually take on a character akin to superstition. He identified the institutions as a set of established rights, obligations, perquisites, and vested interests that grow out of certain axioms of law and custom. The axioms in turn are based on particular conditions that prevail at a given time. Feudalism, for example, started from the conditions of chaos and insecurity prevailing after the fall of Rome. Laws and customs were created, based upon the need for security. Finally, structures were established that enhanced the rights, perquisites, and power of those at the top of the institutional structure. When these underlying conditions change, Veblen argued, the rights and privileges of such vested interests will change more slowly. The laws and axioms that hold together the established order "become superstitions when the scope and method of workday knowledge has outgrown that particular range of preconceptions out of which these make-believe axioms are constructed."[10] The stories a society tells about itself tend to change more slowly than the reality of that society. Building new institutions will be a slow process: "And this will particularly be true when the reconstruction of unseasonable institutions runs counter to a settled and honorable code of ancient principles and a stubborn array of vested interests. . . ."[11]

The values that dominate a society may be widely held. Such values will most often lead to the development of institutional structures that support the values and their continued observance and belief. The development of feudalism is an example of this process. However, in the later stages of feudalism the institutional structures continued to exist and wield power even though the need for security receded. The dominant values of the society, as expressed in its institutional structures and its stories, were held only by a relative few. Those few had sufficient power through the institutional structures to maintain their privilege in the face of changing values.

Veblen's analysis demonstrates that institutions are capable of existing and maintaining their power even after they have outlived their original purposes. As in the transfiguration story, the old order stands fast and resists the breaking in and breaking up occasioned by the new. Indeed, one of the important themes of the rest of this book will be the existence of institutional structures that once served the general interest but now serve only vested interests. These institutions, the values they support, and the stories that support them, stand in the way of social and economic changes that would lead to the actualization of human freedom and to a broader distribution of the fruits of production and the perquisites of power.

C. Stories and the American Experience

When the focus turns to the United States, the same issues emerge. What stories have we told about ourselves, and how have these stories contributed to our values formation and our institutional structures? The issue of the "fit" of these institutions with current social needs will be explored here and will also be the subject of more rigorous analysis in chapter 4.

Two dominant types of stories fill our children's imaginations and help to form their attitudes. There are the hard work/success stories of which the Horatio Alger tales are archetypal. Similar examples are rife, ranging from sports heroes to the Hardy Boys. The frontier is the focus of the other important group of stories. These center upon the overcoming of tremendous obstacles by individuals as a part of the westward movement of the eighteenth and nineteenth centuries. Both of these groups of stories emphasize the importance of hard work, of seizing opportunities, of doing one's best, and of using one's talents to the fullest. In the hard work/success stories, the reward for exemplary conduct is usually monetary success—and always adulation, peer respect, and improved status. The United States is characterized as a place where hard work is rewarded by personal advancement.

Galbraith has pointed out that the hard work of the individual entrepreneur, his employees, the small farmer, the housewife, and other individual participants in the economic and social system takes on such an aura of goodness and value that he has called it the Convenient Social Virtue.[12] The inculcation of that value accords status to people whose prime function in the system is to provide personal services. Such services have traditionally been menial and low paying, yet people continue in some of those jobs even though they could choose alternative occupations that are higher paying. The work ethic celebrated in the success stories provides status in place of income and ensures that these vital services will continue to be performed. Galbraith points in particular to the management of household consumption activities by women as a crucial and valuable service which the society receives virtually gratis because of its wide acceptance as a Convenient Social Virtue.[13]

Perhaps more interesting in terms of a uniquely American view of the world are the frontier stories. The restless pioneer or the fur trader moving ever westward in search of new land, new challenges, and new opportunities, is certainly a story that has filled us with pride in our heritage. A whole theory of American development has been constructed around this image. Its most extensive and pervasive form is known as the Turner thesis after its creator, Frederick Jackson Turner, one of the foremost American historians. He argued that the frontier itself, the existence of extensive unowned, unclaimed lands "to the west," was a primary factor shaping the development of the American economic system. The eastern seaboard avoided extensive pressures because excess population was always moving west. People who were dissatisfied with their economic, social, or political lot could and did move to the lands of opportunity. The West served the additional function of maintaining a higher level of wages in the East because of the western outlet for labor. Employers in the nascent industrial enterprises had to compete with the opportunities that the workers faced in the West; therefore, employers had to maintain reasonable wages if they hoped to continue to employ qualified workers.[14] This vision of the West is sometimes called the "safety valve" theory of westward expansion.

Unqualified belief in the role of the frontier is built into virtually all of the frontier stories. Much of the support for America as the land of opportunity stems from the view of the frontier as a source of incredible riches for the person bold enough to move west and seize them. The focus is on the stories of frontiersmen like Daniel Boone, who discovered the Cumberland Gap and opened up the riches of Kentucky and the West for the land-hungry people of the eastern seaboard. This is the Daniel Boone who founded Boonesboro and made huge new tracts of land available while keeping the Indians at bay. Curiously, the story never details the Daniel Boone who died penniless and landless, cheated out of all of his holdings by greedy land speculators who had a better understanding of the laws of land ownership and possession than did Boone.[15]

Turner's thesis about the frontier has been disproven by modern historians. The pioneers who opened up the West were rarely persons who had been squeezed out by population growth in the East. In fact, there does not seem to be any truth to the notion that population growth was putting pressure on eastern cities. The burgeoning eastern industries were able to absorb almost any increase in population into the active labor force. If anything, labor shortage was the critical problem. Nor does the notion of the safety valve seem very appropriate; the dissatisfied in the East were almost always at the bottom of the income distribution and did not have the resources required for the long trek to the frontier. Indeed, the worse the economic conditions in the East, the more formidable was the cost of moving west.[16] Economic historians are convinced that virtually all settlement of new areas in the West was accomplished by people in the immediately contiguous areas already settled in the East. It was accomplished both by families moving several times during their lifetimes and by succeeding generations moving ever westward.[17] The restlessness of the pioneers caused their movement, not the alleged riches of the West.

Despite all this evidence to the contrary, the frontier hypothesis lives on; the frontier stories have a powerful impact on our own vision of our history. It is a functional belief that allows us to focus on "opportunity" and "potential." Coupled with the hard work/success stories, it blinds us to the lack of opportunity and stunted potential that afflict large segments of our population. As long as these stories prevail, it is easy to explain individual failure as a result of not trying hard enough or of failing to seize opportunity. The onus falls on the failed individual, not on the institutional structures that may have prevented the individual from succeeding.

In many of the American stories, success in *business* is the reward for individual behavior that is oriented around the values of unbounded opportunity and hard work. As a consequence, the pursuit of personal gain plays the dominant role; the good of the society is, at best, subordinate. These stories do not tell the whole story. While the United States may be a land of boundless opportunity, it is available to only some segments of the population; other groups have been systematically excluded. To understand the incompleteness of the stories, we need to look at the impact the American economic system has on some excluded groups. There is another story that describes the reality of existence for many Americans.

Certainly, when we think of economic opportunity, the acquisition of income and wealth is one of the principal issues. Data for the United States show that systematic exclusion of women, blacks, and other minorities has created a severe income discrepancy between their households and those headed by white males. Tables 1 and 2 show this.

These data reveal that women, blacks, and Spanish-origin minorities, in comparison with white males, have consistently had a much smaller share of the income generated by the American economic system. The point is reinforced by the poverty statistics presented in table 3.

TABLE 1

**Median Family Incomes in Current Dollars by Sex and Ethnic Origin,
Selected Years**

	Years				
Family Head	1950	1960	1970	1977	1979
All	$ 3,319	$ 5,620	$ 9,867	$16,009	$19,684
White	3,445	5,835	10,236	16,740	20,524
Black	1,869	3,230	6,516	10,142	12,358
Spanish Origin	. . . . .	. . . . .	. . . . .	10,647	12,566
Male	3,435	5,857	10,480	17,517	. . . . .
Female	1,922	2,968	5,093	7,765	. . . . .

Source: U.S. Department of Commerce, Bureau of the Census, *Statistical Abstract of the United States,* 1978, tables 729, 736, 747; 1980, tables 745, 748.

TABLE 2

Mean Family Income by Sex and Race, 1977

	Race		
Family Head	All	White	Black
Male	$19,686	$20,047	$15,190
Female	9,811	10,947	6,959

Source: *Statistical Abstract of the United States,* 1978, table 741.

TABLE 3

**Percentage of Family Incomes Falling below the Poverty Level by Sex and Race,
1970, 1976, 1977, 1978**

| Family Head | Percent below Poverty within Each Group | | | |
	1970	1976	1977	1978
All	12.6%	11.8%	11.6%	10.1%
White	9.8	9.1	8.9	7.3
Black	32.0	29.4	29.0	29.9
Spanish Origin	.....	.....	22.4	19.8
Male	8.2	7.1	6.9	6.2
Female	38.2	34.4	32.8	34.7

Source: *Statistical Abstract of the United States,* 1978, tables 756, 758; 1980, tables 773, 775.

The generally lower levels of income received by minorities and women lead inexorably to a much greater incidence of poverty among those groups. In addition to income disparities, the conditions of poverty include lower levels of nutrition and much more limited access to quality education and health care. The quality of life is seriously eroded for those forced to live in poverty conditions.

It is not possible to shrug off this high incidence of poverty by assuming that these families are unwilling to work and thus condemn themselves to lower incomes. Table 4

TABLE 4

**Percentage of Poverty Families with at Least One Full-Time Worker, by Sex and
Race, 1975, 1977, 1978**

| Family Head | Percentage with At Least One Full-time Worker | | |
	1975	1977	1978
All			
Male	39.4%	48.0%	46.3%
Female	15.2	13.8	13.8
White			
Male	40.3	48.8	47.9
Female	14.5	11.1	10.4
Black			
Male	34.9	47.3	40.5
Female	16.6	17.3	18.3

Source: *Statistical Abstract of the United States,* 1978, table 765; 1980, table 781.

shows that a high proportion of those whose incomes fall below the poverty level still work full-time. The system prevents many families, particularly those headed by women and minorities, from earning an income even with full-time work that lifts them above poverty.

The incidence of poverty also tends to rise as family heads reach retirement age. Senior citizens living on relatively fixed incomes are particularly susceptible to the inroads of inflation. In recent years they have become another vulnerable minority. Cost-of-living adjustments in social security benefits have helped, but, as table 5 shows, senior citizens still have a higher incidence of poverty than their younger counterparts.

TABLE 5
Percentage of Families with Heads over 65 Having Income below the Poverty Level, by Sex and Race, 1970, 1976, 1977, 1978

Family Head	Percentage below Poverty Level			
	1970	1976	1977	1978
All	22.6%	15.0%	14.1%	14.0%
White	14.6	13.2	11.9	12.1
Black	47.7	34.8	36.3	33.9
Male	15.9	8.0	7.8	7.7
Female	20.1	14.4	13.7	12.1

Source: *Statistical Abstract of the United States*, 1978, table 767; 1980, table 776.

The existence of poverty and low incomes within various groups in the society is exacerbated by unemployment. Those groups already disadvantaged by past and current discrimination, low-quality education, and age can at best compete for only the lowest-paid jobs in the industrial or service fields. They are also the first to feel the impact of unemployment. Sometimes such unemployment results from overt discrimination, but quite often it represents a failure by the system to create enough jobs for less-skilled people. Past discrimination has left them in a position where they cannot compete effectively. Even without current discrimination the system will continue to reject them

TABLE 6
Labor Force Participation Rates and Unemployment Rates by Race and Sex,
1960, 1970, 1977, 1979

	Labor Force Participation Rates				Unemployment Rates			
	All Males	Black Males	All Females	Black Females	All Males	Black Males	All Females	Black Females
1960	84.0%	83.0%	37.8%	48.2%	5.4%	10.7%	5.9%	9.4%
1970	80.6	77.6	43.4	49.5	4.4	7.3	5.9	9.3
1977	78.3	72.2	48.5	51.0	6.2	12.4	8.2	14.0
1979	77.9	70.7	51.5	53.1	5.1	10.3	6.8	12.3

Source: *Statistical Abstract of the United States*, 1978, table 645; 1980, tables 653, 654, 655.

because of this lack of marketable skills. The uneven incidence of unemployment can be seen in tables 6 and 7.

As table 6 shows, labor force participation rates differ somewhat on the basis of race and extensively on the basis of sex. Black males have a somewhat lower percentage of their population entering the labor force. In other words, some significant portion of the black male population is not counted in the labor force or in the employment/unemployment statistics. Even given this, a much higher percentage of the black male labor force is unemployed. The same can be said in comparing the total female labor force to the total male labor force. Thus, the unemployment data may understate the employment problems of blacks and women.

The seniority systems used by most employers and unions mean that unemployment and thus low incomes and poverty are visited much more heavily upon younger workers than upon middle-aged ones. Table 7 shows the disparity in those unemployment figures and points out the tremendously disproportionate effect that such a system has on young blacks.

Income, poverty, and employment differentials have their effects upon the quality of life in both material and psychological terms. The disadvantaged groups find themselves with much less ability to own and use various goods and services that are widely possessed by the white middle class. They also are powerless to do anything to change

TABLE 7
Unemployment by Age, Race, and Sex, 1979

| | Unemployment Rates | | | | | |
| | All | | White | | Other races | |
Age Group	Male	Female	Male	Female	Male	Female
Total	5.1%	6.8%	4.4%	5.9%	10.3%	12.3%
16–19	15.8	16.4	13.9	13.9	31.5	35.7
20–24	8.6	9.6	7.4	7.8	17.0	20.8
25–34	4.2	6.4	3.6	5.6	8.6	11.0
35–44	2.9	4.6	2.5	4.2	5.8	7.0
45–54	2.7	3.9	2.5	3.7	5.2	4.9
55–64	2.7	3.2	2.5	3.0	4.8	4.6
over 65	3.5	3.3	3.1	3.1	6.3	4.6

Source: *Statistical Abstract of the United States,* 1980, table 658.

these material conditions. The stories about the "land of opportunity" simply do not fit their world. Changes in human consciousness without corresponding changes in structures cancels their aspirations. "Wild, irrational hope" cannot prevail if the existing order continues to dominate. The terrible weight of the present maldistribution of income and jobs forecloses on their future and leaves them locked into conditions they can neither control nor change.

It is not just disadvantaged groups who feel the impact of the maldistribution of income and jobs. One of the sources of income out of reach for the bulk of the population is property or asset ownership. The amassing of rental, dividend, or interest income requires the possession of assets. The data for property and asset ownership in the United States show a fairly consistent pattern for the last quarter century. Almost 25 percent of the personal wealth is held by 1 percent of the population. Economic power in the form of wealth is concentrated within a small segment of the population. Therefore, while many of us may not face poverty, and indeed may be quite comfortable, we are relatively powerless to effect any real change in the system. We do not possess the necessary wealth, and therefore we have no power.

This picture of the powerlessness of a very large segment

of the population will be reinforced when we explore the role of the large corporations and other bureaucracies within the social system. One example lends currency to this argument. Despite our affluence, much of the American middle class is being discomfited by the soaring prices and increasing unavailability of gasoline and other petroleum products. We are powerless to affect the decisions of the large oil companies and of the energy bureaucracy.

The promise of the American stories is one of unlimited opportunity for all, but the reality of the American experience is often far different from the promise of its stories.

D. American Institutions

This tension between promise and reality in America shows that our professed values and ideals are not the ones that have formed the current fabric of the American social and economic systems. To understand our system it will be helpful to develop a short history of institutional structures in the United States. The emphasis will be on the economic institutions, but parallel developments were occurring within the social and political institutions.

From the earliest colonization of what is now the eastern United States, the country was blessed with abundant natural resources. Furthermore, the previous experiences of the early settlers often led to the existence or the quick development of technical expertise. The serious shortages were raw labor and capital.

Initially, the shortage of labor was solved by a system of indentured servants and slaves. As labor needs grew and as the location of economic activity became more mobile and more widely spread, there were large waves of immigrants encouraged by the promise of greater economic opportunity and personal freedom. The stories of the American frontier and its opportunities played an important role in attracting the immigrants. The consequent growth of the unskilled and semiskilled labor force, coupled with industrial development, gave rise to a system of wage labor. This created and fed the distinctions between craft and industrial labor in ways that prevented a unified labor movement until well into the twentieth century. Despite the existence of the frontier, history has shown that most members of this labor force were trapped in the eastern cities because they did not have the resources needed to move west. Thus, an unorganized urban labor force with limited economic and geographic mobility was the ultimate solution to the labor shortage.

The interaction of these forces has made the American labor movement much less of a revolutionary force than its counterparts in Europe and other parts of the world. Unions in the United States have been content to get their piece of the action and have avoided real confrontation with the institutional structures that determine, affect, and define our economic system. Our labor movement, particularly in the twentieth century, has had a blue-collar orientation and yet has excluded laboring class people such as blacks and women. Labor has bought into the American story rather than trying to change it.

The early capital shortages were dealt with initially by encouraging the inflow of foreign capital. The immense opportunity presented by the natural resources and existing technological base attracted that capital. As the economic system developed, a set of financial institutions emerged that helped channel individual savings and business profits into further capital expansion. The financial institutions developed almost exclusively to serve a rapidly expanding, market-oriented, free-enterprise economic system. There was virtually no central government until 1789, and even long after that the financial institutions strongly resisted any efforts at regulation or control. Even today we have an almost exclusively private financial system. Virtually no institutionalized mechanisms exist for channeling public credit resources into the private sector—or even from one public sector treasury to another. In another society, the loans from the federal government to Lockheed, Penn Central, and New York City would have been made with ease. The real control of money and credit availability rests almost exclusively with a group of private sector institutions. They make decisions in line with their own best interests, rather than having credit availability serve the public interest.

The industrial and commercial enterprises that emerged in the colonies and in the early United States were almost exclusively owner-operated single proprietorships or partnerships. The enterprises were small and faced a reasonable degree of competition. The limited-liability corporation became more important with the necessity of gathering large sums of capital and spreading risk. The increased scale of operation needed to efficiently exploit natural resources and technological expertise further contributed to the increasing size of business enterprises. Still, such corporations were controlled by their owners through a board of directors and almost always had a dominant owner as manager. This combination left most enterprises reasonably competitive and reasonably responsive to market signals. Under these conditions, the interests of the consumer and of the society at large were served effectively, although certainly not perfectly. The American story and the American reality were not totally out of sync.

The Declaration of Independence and the Bill of Rights are axial documents in both United States and world history for describing and clarifying individual rights. Among the most important principles defined in the documents are the importance of the individual and of the individual's right to own, use, and dispose of property or wealth. Several legislative actions and judicial rulings in the nineteenth century extended those same rights to that institutional "person," the business corporation. That fact, coupled with the industrial growth accompanying the technological revolutions of the eighteenth and nineteenth centuries, led to rapid expansion of industrial corporations and vast accumulations of property. Economic power became concentrated in corporations.[18] By the beginning of the twentieth century, ownership and management functions were being separated. The owner-managed business enterprise was becoming the exception. The increasing size of industrial corporations and the necessity to spread risk made it infeasible for one person or family to control an enterprise. The increased economic power caused by expansion and accumulation accrued to the corporation and hired managers, not to the people who owned the corporation. The power of such accumulation rests in the ability to wield it effectively to achieve various ends and goals. As corporations expanded, the decision-making problems became so complex that only professional managers, fully cognizant of all of the issues, could make competent decisions.[19] Thus the power to use the accumulated wealth was weaned away from its nominal owners and put in the hands of a professional managerial class.

The result is that corporate management becomes cloaked in an aura of expertise and insulated from close scrutiny. The sheer size of industrial enterprises in our contemporary world enables them to protect themselves from the market. The oil companies can manipulate the market because they control so much of the flow of petroleum resources. That prevents us, as consumers, from using the market mechanism to force them to accede to our needs. Consumer and public interests need not be served by corporate management. The important societal value that has traditionally been accorded to the individual and personal property rights has accrued to the large corporations. This prevents effective regulatory action that might turn the corporation to the regular service of the common good.

In economic terms, we have a situation in which large organizations and large corporations have a vested interest in the existing system. Despite the stories and the values that have formed our American heritage, power in the economic, political, and social spheres rests with large organizations and their management, not with individuals. As a result, these vested interests stand as obstacles to societal change and limit the impact of new values.

There is an inherent tension between the values that are expressed in these American stories and the actual experience of American society. We are not truly a "land of opportunity" unless we are a land of opportunity for all. Our values have perhaps become Veblen's superstitions. They serve the vested interests by holding up and maintaining our belief in an ideal that cannot be realized in the current context. The power of that ideal can be used to make the disaffected feel a sense of personal, existential responsibility and guilt for their lack of success. Such a move bleeds off the potential power of unity among the disaffected. It prevents them from realizing the dominant role that systematic structures play in maintaining their disadvantaged and powerless conditions. There is no promise of an open future within the existing order. Without the vision of a new future we can only live *in* our circumstances. We cannot rise *above* and live *against* those circumstances. We are cut off from any stories that challenge the power of the existing order.

Notes

1. David C. McClelland, *The Achieving Society* (New York: Free Press, 1961), p. 76.
2. Ibid., p. 40.
3. Ibid., p. 41.
4. Ibid., p. 43.
5. Ibid., p. 43.
6. Ibid., pp. 43–44.
7. Ibid., pp. 50–56.
8. Ibid., pp. 63–70.
9. Ibid., pp. 97 and 102.
10. Thorstein Veblen, *The Vested Interests and the Common Man* (New York: Viking Press, 1946), p. 33.
11. Ibid., p. 34.
12. John Kenneth Galbraith, *Economics and the Public Purpose* (Boston: Houghton Mifflin, 1973), p. 30.
13. Ibid., pp. 33–37.
14. Frederick Jackson Turner, *The Frontier in American History* (New York: Holt, Rinehart and Winston, 1920), p. 259.

15. Jared Sparks, *The Library of American Biography,* vol. 13 (Boston: Little, Brown, 1847), pp. 158–60.
16. Herman E. Krooss, *American Economic Development,* 3rd ed. (Englewood Cliffs, N.J.: Prentice-Hall, 1974), pp. 102–5.
17. Ibid.
18. George A. Steiner, *Government's Role in Economic Life* (New York: McGraw-Hill, 1953), pp. 103–6.
19. Galbraith, *Economics and the Public Purpose,* p. 82.

3   The American Story

Both individuals and nations understand, integrate, and function through stories. The significance of the national experience is inevitably shared among ourselves and conveyed to the world in narrative form. The most common feature is language gleaned from religious tradition. The American story takes the form of a civil religion.

From the beginning the imagery of faith has been drawn upon to explain what we are as a nation. The first settlers gravitated to the biblical notion of a people "connected to the purposes of God." Our coinage has borne the phrase "In God We Trust" and in the 1950s the pledge of allegiance was amended to affirm "one nation under God." However superficial or even trivial that may seem, the antecedents are rich and deep. Religious symbols answer questions of purpose and destiny, speak of "what is" and "what ought to be," and explain how our lives connect with the divine. Americans have seldom been reluctant to draw upon those symbols for their own purposes. The authors of the Constitution proclaimed that our "inalienable rights" are derived from a divine creator. The preservation of those rights depends upon them being more than the creation of human minds. The notion of a divine hand in the affairs of the nation is ratified consistently in the inaugural addresses of presidents. George Washington referred to the "great Author of every public and private good." Thomas Jefferson spoke of "that Divine power in whose hands we are." James Madison referred to "that almighty Being whose power regulates the destiny of nations." More recently, President Kennedy concluded with the words, "let us go forth to lead the land we love, asking His blessing and His help, but knowing that here on earth God's work must truly be our own."[1] As a nation we have understood ourselves both horizontally and vertically; our story has been one of both human initiative and divine intention.

One of the more obvious needs of society is for an "intentional horizon,"[2] a goal or *telos* that enables it to distinguish "what is" from "what ought to be." No society can grow and intensify its possibilities without a controlling vision. The future tense is essential for overcoming the inertia and aimlessness of present times. Integration, cohesion, and dynamism occur because a people relate themselves to a horizon and live under the jurisdiction of that future. The existing order and its institutions remain viable only in the measure they are at the service of a humanly desirable vision. Durkheim refers to this process as "idealizing . . . substituting for the real world another different one."[3] This formation of the ideal is not something apart from society but remains part of it. The process is indigenous even though its results do not correspond to the actualities at hand. The ideals give the society unity and personality.

Once one begins to think of "an intentional horizon," the social processes open in the direction of religion. Durkheim contends that "this systematic idealization is an essential characteristic of religion."[4] Memory and anticipation are primary functions of religious beliefs and rituals. The promises that come to function at the heart of faith are drawn from what has been and connect with what will be. Both remembering and anticipating are futurizing processes. Knowing who makes the promises conditions our confidence that they will be honored. Religion addresses the need of individuals and society because it is "that symbol system which provides man with an ultimate view of reality; a basic interpretative scheme; a cultural system that answers fundamental questions about the purpose and destiny of his life; a set of unique symbols that tells him the way things are and by implication the way they should be."[5] Religion gives shape and form and substance to the intentional horizon. Without that society would wilt and finally self-destruct.

Whatever the society is and becomes is directly related to human initiative conditioned by the intentional horizon. Human activity and reflection are the source of the intentional horizon's formation. At the same time, human beings are products of the society they develop. Once this creation is established it is formative—and formidable in its capacity to shape humankind. Thus we have in society what Peter Berger calls "world construction"—a process in which "an ordering of experience" occurs in a meaningful way.[6] World construction saves individuals and society from chaos and disorientation and places them significantly in the universe.

This process in its most intense form is again essentially religious. Human ordering is not perceived as grounded merely in our own sense of what is possible but in some ultimate. Without bypassing humankind and its initiatives, there are believed to be "powerful forces" operative in history that are determined to enable human beings to live meaningfully in the universe. "Religion is the audacious attempt to conceive of the entire universe as being humanly significant."[7] It functions in such a way as to provide "a sacred cosmos."[8] To have a sacred canopy is to be confident that the ordering of our existence individually and collectively is not capricious but grounded in the divine order of things. The stability of existence is a function of its correspondence to a larger scheme of things rather than simply to human aspiration and illusion. The framework for our lives singularly and together is finally not our own. Thus religion brings to society its "intentional horizon" and in the larger context provides a significance that is durable and true.

A. Civil Religion in America

The premise of American civil religion is that we have always constructed our national story with religious symbols. There are at least three types of American civil religion. It is important to draw some clear distinctions and specify how the term will function here.

The first type is entirely descriptive. It is concerned with identifying the American way of life without any normative framework. The careful examination of the "is" is done without any reference to an "ought to be." This is perceived by Richey and Jones in their introduction to *American Civil Religion* as a folk religion. "By examining the actual life, ideas, values, ceremonies, and loyalties of the people, conclusions are drawn as to the existence and status of civil religion. The starting point is . . . what actually is on the basis of surveys, polls, and empirical studies."[9] Religion and the life of the nation are indistinguishable. Religion *is* the life of the nation—that common faith which binds and energizes.

Will Herberg was an especially astute student of this version. His concern was with an organic structure that emerges from the existence of the folk. Civil religion has developed naturally as a faith common to Americans and functions indigenously in their lives. Its effect is to afford national unity without any discordant element. In a very real sense for Herberg, American civil religion is a religionizing of the American experience: "national life is apotheosized, national values are religionized, national heroes are divinized, national history is experienced as a *Heilsgeschichte,* as a redemptive history."[10] This folk religion is marked by a remarkable sense of purpose in history, liturgies and a liturgical year as evidenced by national holidays and saints (Washington, Lincoln, Roosevelt, and Kennedy—each with his own shrine), and spirituality in the form of an idealism about ourselves and our unique possibilities.

American civil religion, then, is the way in which we project ourselves as we are onto the larger screen. It has a celebratory and sustaining impact but not a self-critical one, and the study of it is a tracing process, not one that comes from a transcendent claim.

A second meaning of American civil religion is a self-serving nationalism. It then has a normative component but still not a critical one. There is no real transcendent feature, even when the vocabulary of transcendence is broadly evident. Patriotism itself may become a deity. The national faith is proscriptive, and therefore performs a normative function. The sense of "ought to be" is invoked, but in a way that leads to adulation and enshrinement. The nation is God and patriotism is the deification process. But since the only transcendence is self-transcendence, the norm is restricted to claims that have already been met and that will be continued. There is no source of strain from without that occasions overwhelming obligation. Therefore, there cannot finally be an objective critical element. Any semblance of critical apparatus is generated from within the nation's vision of itself.

Self-serving nationalism as a civil religion can take both a personal and a public form. The personal form is exemplified by Richard Nixon and carefully examined by Charles P. Henderson. President Nixon had an inordinate capacity to wrap himself in the flag, piously bow his head, and point to God. Worship services in the East Room of the White House were a form of that. While his use of religious language was restrained, his symbolic acts had the same effect. His association with Billy Graham and Norman Vincent Peale—and especially his mysterious appearance at a Graham Crusade in the midst of a campaign—had the effect of drawing a religious mantle around himself. He knew the "heart of America" and it was "good." In the context of Vietnam and Watergate, that was an astonishing profession of national innocence. The overtones were religious—if not biblical. Henderson points out that even when Nixon appropriated language that alluded to a transcendent and might have been the basis of a critical framework, he emptied the terms of their meaning until they served his purpose. "Nixon systematically appropriates the vocabulary of the church—faith, trust, hope, belief, spirit—and applies these words not to a transcendent God but to his own nation, and worse, to his personal vision of what that nation should be. . . . Lacking a transcendent God, he seems to make patriotism his religion, the American dream his deity."[11]

There is a more public version of this national self-worship as well. It differs from the personal only in that it is shared and is not an extension of a personal vision. It is a "zealous nationalism" that embraces both our innocence as a people and our mission to redeem the world. The hidden agenda is to make the world safe for *us*. The national life takes the form of a crusade and a willingness to articulate high purposes and implement them through venal means. Herman Melville caught the spirit of it when he wrote: "Since we bear the ark of the liberties of the world, it is clear that the political Messiah . . . has come in *us*." As Robert Jewett sees so clearly, "The consequence, as Melville put it, is that deeds which ordinarily would be classified as 'national selfishness' are acceptable, since they enhance the glory and power of the messianic people. 'We cannot do a good to America but we give alms to the world.' "[12] The nation is believed to be free of selfish ends in the goal of saving the world—and that is the ultimate expression of its self-worship. Thus, the second brand of American civil religion sustains and exalts the nation and frees it from self-doubt.

The third meaning of American civil religion is as a religion of the nation that aspires to be authentically normative and embraces a critical function. It is an understanding that attempts to do justice to both the priestly and prophetic components of religion. The priestly element is "celebrative, affirmative, culture-building."[13] It engages in rituals and affirmations that give cohesion to the nation and yield meaning and identity to the people. The prophetic element is judgmental: a dialectic is sustained between "what is" and "what ought to be." And that is occasioned by the sense that there is a transcendent reality which stands over and against the actualization of our national life. The nation is "under God" rather than under its own self-understanding. The biblical God is at large as the source of our sense of justice and righteousness. Both solidarity and disparity are embraced by this religion of the nation. Robert Bellah is the most conspicuous example of this view of civil religion, and his emphasis upon the priestly and prophetic element is evident in the often articulated claim that "the God of American civil religion is the God of Abraham, Isaac and Jacob." It is this later brand that will dominate our examination now; Bellah's meaning will control our understanding of the term.

B. Robert Bellah and American Civil Religion

American civil religion, a la Bellah, came into being in 1967 with the publication of an article in *Daedalus*. From that time on it became "a social fact." As an interpretation it drew together distinctive features of the American experience and from then on held its own. In Bellah's words "the very currency of the notion of civil religion is the earnest of its reality."[14]

American civil religion is a useful construct, sustained by an elaborate mythical structure, which focuses the religious meaning Americans have found in their experience. It draws upon the biblical symbols of "Exodus, Chosen People, Promised Land, New Jerusalem, Sacrificial Death and Rebirth" as a means of national self-understanding.[15] It is "an understanding of the American experience in the light of ultimate and universal reality."[16] Institutionally it has no alliances or antagonisms with the churches and synagogues of the land. American civil religion exists beside them and outside them. It is a common faith that animates and explains the nation to itself without falling victim to self-adulation or equivalence to the American way of life. Rather, "there actually exists alongside of and rather clearly differentiated from the churches an elaborate and well-institutionalized civil religion in America."[17] Americans, Bellah argues, have always given a religious meaning to our national life, and American civil religion is the more formal articulation of its existence.

One of Bellah's most frequent references is to a sermon preached by John Winthrop in 1630 aboard a ship heading for the new land. Winthrop was later to become the first governor of the Massachusetts Bay Colony. In the sermon the governor interprets the venture in a theistic framework: "We have entered into covenant with Him [God] for this work, we have taken out a commission. The Lord has given us leave to draw our own articles. Now if the Lord shall please to hear us, and bring us in peace to the place we desire, then hath he ratified this covenant and sealed our commission [and] will expect a strict performance of the articles contained in it . . ."[18] It would have been easy for them to interpret the whole venture horizontally, i.e., "we are a band of people alienated from our homeland who seek a new land in which we can establish our own ways." But they understood themselves as entering into a contract with God, having a mission of which God might approve, and incurring obligation to God. Obviously this event does not stand as evidence in its own right; it is paradigmatic and can be seen as reflecting an understanding of the American experience in a religious context. This sense of contract with and obligation to God appears again in presidential inauguration speeches, the framing of the Declaration of Independence, and the sense of a communal ethic at large. The obligation to carry out God's will on earth echoes through national events from the words and acts of the founders to the most recent addresses of contemporary presidents. While it is not worship of the American experience, American civil religion does draw together what is worthy in that experience.

In a later book, *The Broken Covenant,* Bellah gives more substance to the argument. He considers in detail the sense of origin that shaped our founding, the sense of being a chosen people that shaped our destiny, and the sense of salvation that shaped our relation to the world.

Dr. Bellah has been remarkably free of a need to refine

his 1967 claim in the succeeding decade, but he does refer
to "a certain ambiguity in my original article," which is
worth pursuing because it distinguishes his work from the
work of others.[19] The ambiguity is lifted by drawing a distinction between "special civil religion" and "general civil
religion." The latter has as its essence "the lowest common
denominator of church religions."[20] It is a form of natural
religion that emerges from "the hearts of all mankind" and
provides a faith that facilitates government. A conspicuous
example is the much quoted remark of President
Eisenhower: "Our government makes no sense unless it is
founded in a deeply felt religious faith—and I don't care
what it is." By contrast, special civil religion is normative
and draws unreservedly upon biblical imagery and understanding. It is not all-inclusive but affirms the god under
whom the nation lives to be the same god as that of Abraham, Isaac, and Jacob. Bellah concludes, "only the biblical
religions, I venture to think, can provide the energy and
vision for a new turn in American history, perhaps a new
understanding of covenant, which may be necessary not
only to save ourselves but to keep us from destroying the
rest of the world."[21]

C. Critiques of American Civil Religion

The most obvious question as one reflects critically upon
American civil religion is: Does it really exist? Bellah's
answer that it exists because it is functioning as a conceptual tool has to be at least partially persuasive. That claim is
substantiated by the books and conferences that take it as a
theme. It is, indeed, a "social fact" and as such is very
much present in our collective existence. Beyond that, it is
very difficult to refute the claim that "biblical imagery provided the basic framework for imaginative thought in
America up until quite recent times and, unconsciously, its
control is still formidable."[22] The biblical myths live in the
American culture and are readily appropriated as analogies

through which to translate the meaning of our experience. To be an American would seem to involve a vision of ourselves as a pilgrim people in search of a viable order and sustained by the faith that while God's will is not necessarily our own, we are at least informed by it. It would seem fair to operate on the premise that something like an American civil religion is present yielding direction, cohesion, and meaning to our national life. The more telling issue then becomes how we should value it and respond to it.

Three points need to be made. The first has to do with the phenomenon of lending symbols. The use of images with a specific transcendent content outside the orbit where their meaning is definite and controlled certainly leads to a dilution of meaning. To the community of faith the symbols are not merely related to a "something" big up there but to the "God of Abraham, Isaac and Jacob" and "the Crucified One." The easy lending policy enables politicians, and essentially political cultic ceremonies like Memorial Day services, to draw freely upon words initially defined in relation to sacred content. "During most of American history the churches have been a ready lender of the signals of transcendence. In the last decade or so they have become . . . somewhat more jealous of the symbols they can still call theirs, and somewhat more reluctant to see them debased."[23]

It might be argued that there is a natural alliance between the journey toward freedom in the Exodus and the American posture in world affairs. But they are not the same story. At the very least there is some ambiguity in the designation of liberators and oppressors, which our experience in Vietnam calls into question. The link between the Israelites and Americans is tenuous, and to lend terms like *chosen people* to the American experience is eventually to depreciate their meaning. It is difficult, finally, to resist the conclusion that American civil religion is involved in symbol manipulation, the preemption of context which enables a casual transposing of symbols from their original environment to a different situation. Reflecting on another context, John Wilson of Princeton makes a telling point: "*Ad Hoc God* illusions simply do not constitute a theology; there must be some consistent exploration of relevant issues in such a way that a frame of reference oriented to the deity or to the more fundamental premises of a culture—whatever the particular coloration—has a logical status or plays an effective and shaping role."[24]

The second point has to do with the capacity of American civil religion to mediate the prophetic element. There is a sense in which it is best suited for the role of maintenance and the assurance of legitimacy. Institutions work against the process of alienation, the process in which communities and persons become strange to themselves. Institutions are at their best in domesticating the sense of otherness. One can hardly expect the structures of a society to work toward their own weakening or eventual destruction. Once they begin to impede the actualization of freedom they do not easily begin to self-destruct. Quite the opposite—as was argued in chapter 2—they gear up for self-preservation. Even an "intentional horizon" that has been biblically shaped and formed can be shut down to a point where it gives no more than a comfortable nudge to the present order. Bellah can argue that American civil religion can judge as well as comfort. In a sense it can, but it is better equipped for the one task than the other. The social construction of reality through civil religion will inevitably sacrifice the prophetic component first. Because it emerges from the American experience and is naively related to biblical images, the power of those images to transform is constrained at best and inoperative at worst. Lived experience stands against a new future that would disrupt the present. Any setting of a coming kingdom against the actuality of a present society will give rise to inevitable conflicts and disruption of functions. "In our preliminary moment of history, antagonisms are indispensable for bringing present forms under criticism and for pointing to new possibilities for reordering of the human community."[25] That, alas, is not a process likely to be mediated by a civil religion grounded in our experience of ourselves as a nation.

These two points are themselves preliminary and their strength is intensified and legitimatized by another concern that focuses on Bellah's contention that the "God of Abraham, Isaac and Jacob" is the God of American civil religion. This is perhaps the point at which the difference between American history and sacred history becomes most evident. How specific and substantive can transcendence be when it is set to the purposes of a civil religion? Herbert Richardson argues, and Robert Bellah appears to agree, "it is essential that the transcendence which is a constitutive part of the democratic process remains symbolically empty, for particularity of content would operate to prevent precisely the openness it is meant to guarantee."[26] Inevitably it would seem that the God of American civil religion would function to serve the nation. Only in the most limited sense could that God have the specificity of God revealed in Jesus Christ, crucified and risen. The crucifixion and resurrection are instruments of displacement; they set the tension between the "is" and the "ought" in a way that "what is" cannot tolerate or support.

It was not a theologian but a U.S. senator who identified the problem for public consumption. At a national prayer breakfast on February 1, 1973, in Washington, Mark Hatfield warned: "beware of the real danger of misplaced allegiance, if not outright idolatry, to the extent we fail to distinguish between the God of American civil religion and the God who reveals Himself in Holy Scripture and in Jesus Christ. [Civil religion is] faith . . . in a small and exclusive deity, a loyal spiritual Advisor to power and prestige, a Defender of only the American nation, the object of a national folk religion devoid of moral content." Hatfield later proceeded to call for acts of national repentence. (Never mind that both contexts were themselves at least bordering on civil religion.) He was alert to the vulnerability of American civil religion to a takeover in the content of its transcendence.

The litmus test for American civil religion is this: Does it have sufficient content in the concept of transcendence to intercept the forces that would make the nation God? The refusal of deification is not something which comes naturally to societies and their institutions. Only a Transcendent can tell the nation, "You are not God." If, as in the case of American civil religion, the concept of transcendence is in any sense "symbolically empty," that leaves a vacuum for pretenders. When the content is defined by the "Crucified Christ," it will not readily allow a vacuum. The early Christians were considered atheists for good reason. Their image of God was so controlled and conceived by what was revealed in Christ that there was no space for alien allegiances. "For those who recognize the Christ of God in the Crucified one, the glory of God no longer shines on the crown of the mighty, but alone in the face of the Son of Man."[27] And if that event defines what the "actualization of freedom" means, then a liberation process will challenge any forms in which the journey toward freedom is impeded by a civil religion. The evidence that American civil religion can resist accommodation and idolatry is wanting, and the reason appears to be located in its understanding of transcendence.

D. Liberation Theology and American Civil Religion

It might be argued that American civil religion and liberation theology tell the same story. Isn't the scenario for each a journey toward freedom? The American experience began in a flight from restraint. The documents and institutions that emerged from the American Revolution had as their goal the establishment and preservation of freedom. The nation has a self-identity in the world as a beacon for freedom and a guardian of human rights. Under the trusteeship of American civil religion, hasn't the national agenda been the provision of an environment for living in, living above, and living against one's circumstances? This would suggest an overlap of consequence with liberation theology.

One who substantiates that claim is John Coleman.[28] He begins with the contention that civil religion is inevitable. It is "a functional universal: every nation has one."[29] Both individuals and corporate entities struggle with the issues of identity, vocation, and destiny. That places them in the orbit of religion, where one grasps for its symbols and rituals and the provision of legitimacy and justification they offer. Beyond that "national experiences of threat, contingency, breakdown, and possible decline and death bring collectivities to a . . . religious threshold."[30] The resources of faith become the tools for national self-affirmation and healing. A secular state cannot sustain itself for long without immersion in a religious journey.

The issue then becomes one of sorting out authentic from inauthentic versions. For Coleman the criteria are clear.[31] Does the civil religion have a transcendent factor that occasions judgment? Do the symbols and rituals provoke commitment to the best in the nation's history? Is the prophetic strain full and vital? Does patriotism include a concern for human beings beyond our borders? Is a sense of justice sustained by the civil religion? Coleman is echoing Bellah in inviting us to view American civil religion at its best and not argue from inauthentic expressions.

The ultimate thrust of Coleman's thesis is that American civil religion provides liberation theology with a fortuitous and indispensable resource for working out its program. Its principal asset is that it provides liberation theology with a usable past that can engender a viable future. Indeed, he argues, we impair our national agenda if we leave "civil heritage and patriotism to the Yahoos."[32] Beyond that, he claims that "the best strand of America's civil religion is a liberation theology."[33] The task of liberation theology is to tease the usable past into consciousness as a national story and use it to launch a new future for America, and through it, the world.

In order to evaluate Coleman's thesis, we will need to examine civil religion and liberation theology more carefully to determine the degree, if any, of convergence and compatibility. The first comparison is methodological— how do advocates of American civil religion and liberation theology proceed in the development of their position?

Robert Bellah is clear about how one discerns the prospects for the future. The text is the past and the task is to resurrect the vision that has animated the nation. Our destiny is in our conception of our origins and in the prevailing sense of purpose that has fashioned America at its best. Historical data can lead to an understanding of the "American dream" and of our ideals. American civil religion begins in our roots and the value invested in our national existence through religious imagery. We are a people called from exile by God to an uncommon community. It is the force of our past that will renew us and enable a revision of our present. Our possibilities are in a secure relationship to our promise as a nation with a religiously framed self-identity.

The responsibility of the scholar is to aid the process of synchronizing us with our past by drawing it into view. We are lost because there has been an eclipse of the religious meaning of our national life. In order to learn from our past and be transformed by it, the agenda is: "1) that we search the whole tradition from its earliest beginnings. . . 2) that we subject everything we find to the most searching criticism, something that goes far beyond simply distinguishing the good tradition from the bad tradition. . . 3) that we open up our search entirely beyond the ambit of our own tradition."[34] Our praxis is initially intellectual, a reflection upon our past which discerns our best heritage and offers it for the formation of an alternative future.

American civil religion is a theology from above in that it proceeds from a formulation of the ideal to the circumstances at hand in anticipation of a different future. It works into the present from our heritage and toward a recovery of destiny.

The obvious assumption is that putting us in touch with our past has transforming power. Momentum is generated toward the future in the recognition of our heritage. The appeal to what has guided us from the beginning is a remarkable force in overcoming what separates us from our best. When we recognize ourselves we are enabled to be ourselves. Bellah is quick to admit that the functioning of American civil religion can be imperiled; there were recent times in which he could lament that it is winter in America. But "those who have claimed that civil religion is finished may be a bit premature."[35] Writing after the 1972 election and in the trail of Watergate, he held out the hope of 1976 for a rebirth of civil religion, which he now believes to have occurred. American civil religion is a durable phenomenon with an almost limitless availability to resuscitation.

Liberation theologians begin in a different history, the one in which we are living. For them, critical reflection on experience is not a matter of determining the sweep of events or placing them in perspective. That process often dilutes and diminishes. It leads one to say, "well, we are all oppressed in some way," or "things have really gotten better in recent years," or "we have done what we could under the circumstances." Those moves deplete the intensity of the present and mortgage the urgency of the condition of those who suffer. On one level this means there is no advance understanding of truth brought to the situation. On another it means that truth or reality are exposed and present themselves in the particularity of times and events. The text for liberation theology is the conditions at hand. Theology occurs only after "we have tried to comprehend our day-to-day life in history. This would include our economic, political, and cultural life."[36] Theology springs from critical reflection upon what is going on.

Unlike American civil religion this is not an intellectual praxis, a scholar's search for vision and ideals in the action of former times. The place of discernment is the present, but the persons doing the discernment are those getting hurt or those involved in resisting the forces of oppression. The voice is from below—from those on the bottom. There is not only an attempt to synchronize theology with the present age; that has often been the agenda, especially in America. The task is to begin from within the forms of oppression and to name the barriers to freedom. Those who are poor, humiliated, and otherwise oppressed have the only voice that can name the present. The rest of us can only listen and respond. The poor have what Hugo Assmann calls an "epistemological privilege." Only those who suffer the present truly comprehend it. The voice from above diminishes and dilutes. The voice from below knows the pain from which the cry of anguish emerges and before which theology is called to attention. Nothing intercedes to diminish the intensity or complexity.

Liberation theology is not so naive as to deny that oppression has a history. Indeed, that history of oppression sustains the density of the experience and constitutes its sense of permanence. Taking the present as one's text impedes the temptation to diminish the uniqueness of the experience for each oppressed person or to weaken the determination to resist it. Hugo Assmann argues that "our situation is our primary and basic reference point" and goes on to say, "the others—the Bible, tradition, the magisterium or teaching authority of the church, history of dogma, and so on—even though they need to be worked out in contemporary practice, do not constitute a primary source of 'truth in itself' unconnected with the historical 'now' of truth in action."[37] What Assmann is making clear is that liberation theology has a number of contexts but the first voice is that from within pain. The word of God may be heard there for some because it has been heard before, but the authentic hearing of it occurs not in advance but in what lies at hand. "The real epiphany of God's word is the word of the poor man who says, 'I am hungry.' "[38]

The methodological difference between American civil religion and liberation theology is that while the former moves *to* the present with the equipment provided by scholars' reflections on our heritage, the latter moves *from* the intensity and complexity of the present as defined by those in the midst of oppression. How does this distinction affect their stories? In the measure that liberation theology is faithful to its resolve to comprehend the present as experienced by the oppressed, it will tell a story wed to the pain and anguish of the age. The biblical story will be told in explicit and controlling reference to those who are getting hurt. The features of the biblical tradition called into play will be those that collate God's identification with human suffering. The imagery of a suffering God, for example, will be prominent. The tone of the story may have a sturdy component of outrage. The story told by American civil religion will be more gentle in relation to the existing order—and indeed to the present in all its forms. Holding abstractions gleaned from history may have enticing capabilities but it will likely not provoke violent ruptures with the social situation at hand. Ideals have more vulnerability to compromise than does the cry of pain at the hurting edges of experience. We yield a principle more readily than we deny a person.

Perhaps the issue can be shaped somewhat differently. American civil religion functions as what Paul Ricoeur calls an "ideological screen." It filters out. Because American civil religion begins in our identity as conveyed through our heritage, there is a measure of resistance to those realities which do not fit. Given the way we see ourselves, the tendency is to miss the data that work against our national self-perception. We cannot imagine that our government might have complicity in the fall of Chile's President Allende or that our purposes in Vietnam could be anything other than a commitment to freedom. The "cruel innocence" about which Michael Harrington writes may well be occasioned by our civil religion. Our ideology intercepts the cries of pain and the acts of perversion. It may also be that our civil religion fosters what Harrington calls "the *status quo* as utopia." Our sense of ourselves and what ought to be "is a visionary rationalization of present misery."[39] In a real sense, the story told by American civil religion is the story we want told, free of contamination by the actuality of our circumstances. When the formation of the theology is in relation to the voice of suffering, it is a different story—and a different theology.

This is not to argue that American civil religion has no capacity to mediate judgment upon the nation; or that it fails to move the present in new directions. Heritage at its best affects destiny, but perceiving and interpreting the present primarily from the perspective of the past diminishes the cry of pain and discounts in abstractions the anguish of the hurt.

A second comparison is the relation of religion to societal formation and the consequences of that relationship.

Central to American civil religion is the premise that religion functions to integrate and energize the nation. It appeals to spiritual resources for the formation of a communal consciousness and a sense of destiny. The health and preservation of the nation are at the mercy of a civil religion. While some might see this as not more than a public piety, a psychic patriotism, civil religion is too pervasive and fundamental to be merely a rallying point. Clearly, "there is in American society a vague but real cluster of symbols, values, hopes, and intimations of the transcendent which overarch our common life."[40] Their combined effect is to nurture a sense of "peoplehood" without which no nation can survive. Religion thus provides a political service through naming and symbolizing a spiritual foundation. The function of religion in society is remarkably similar to that of faith in the life of the individual.

Given the religion/society model within American civil religion, it is important to explore the phenomenon of Christendom. We are apt to understand that term in relation to Constantine and eras in which the church became a controlling political force. However, the phenomenon has more subtle forms, namely, when Christianity independent of the church is perceived as that which orients the nation.

The church's legitimating powers are at the disposal of the state. Then, the Christian symbols are not used as a restraint but as a blessing. Once the symbols are out on loan to the nation, their function undergoes expansion and the concept of a Christian nation emerges along with Christian politicians and even Christian economics. Certainly American civil religion is not seen by most of its advocates as ending in Christendom. Bellah and others want to maintain its capacity to mediate the prophetic element, the component of critical distance. The provision of a "sacred canopy" is not intended to immunize against criticism or to render inviolate the national practice. Rather, it is intended to enable and release the power of our best. But what follows is a slippery slope: symbols once on loan for integrating soon are turned to sanctioning and then sacralizing. What Peter Berger calls the "world-constructing" and "world-maintaining" functions of religion blend and finally become indistinguishable.

American civil religion works from the premise of religion's functionality in society. Its task is to make the society work. Liberation theology proceeds from a different model. That model need not deny the inevitability of civil religion. Even Jürgen Moltmann concedes that "political religion is found everywhere. A society integrates itself with the help of symbols and a nation represents its origins, its struggles for existence, its destiny and its self-consciousness in mythicized stories."[41] Yet what is crucial in liberation theology is that Christianity leads to the church and not to a Christian nation; its consequence is the formation of a "beloved community" with a critical relation to the society, not the affirmation of the state and the exaltation of its purposes. Authentic Christianity cannot become a culture; the adjective *Christian* can only modify or refer to the content of faith. When one barters the symbols of the content away, there is a process of contamination. The noun takes on a larger meaning and status than it deserves, and the adjective is drained of essential content.

Liberation theology has as its primary agenda the

scrutinizing of self-sacralizing tendencies. It stands in a dialectical relationship to the society—and in particular to its political institutions. The Christian faith authentically proclaimed eschews all alliances with the nation's understanding of itself and the policies that flow from it. Authentic faith strives to identify and dissolve the false convenants that occur. Liberation theology seeks to withdraw biblical symbols from the open market so that they can be used against the state and its pretensions. The force of Christian symbols and rituals must be retained for resistance. Liberation theology ends in a church that says no to the encroachment upon the imagery of the sacred.

The consequences of the story told by American civil religion and liberation theology are substantial. Liberation theology creates a story built upon "the Mosaic themes of conflict, exodus, and promise within human history," while American civil religion builds upon the themes of "harmony, arrival, and fulfillment."[42] Bellah's contention notwithstanding, one story works to sanction and support; the other to disestablish and discomfort. The notion of the religious mediation in the stories is radically different. In American civil religion, religion is bound up with the existing order because of its integral role in creating and sustaining that order. That which has been used to fashion one identity in the life of a nation is not available in full force for the formation of an alternative identity. The transforming power is wasted. Indeed, even sensitivity to the need for a new identity is faint. In liberation theology the focus is upon the formation of a people within the church who are a cognitive minority, "a group of people whose view of the world differs significantly from the one generally taken for granted in their society." It is a community that lives from a body of "deviant knowledge"—the Christian faith.[43] They cannot participate in a process of lending the symbols of deviance for sanctioning. The Gospel creates tension with society; it withholds approval and retains its symbols for a critical function.

American civil religion provides a legitimizing story; it

sanctions "what is" while the ideal of "what ought to be" beckons for attention. Liberation theology provides a delegitimizing story; moving from a version of "what is" defined from below, it summons into force the "what ought to be" of the biblical faith. It sets a new agenda for the nation.

A third comparison centers on the nature of selfhood implicit in and nurtured by American civil religion and liberation theology. Frederick Herzog draws an important distinction between the private and corporate self.[44] The private self takes as its reference point itself, the fulfillment of its possibilities and needs. It is a self that the individual creates, controls, and glories in. Achievement and success are its benchmarks, self-indulgence and narcissism its final destiny. At best, the private self is "man's false relationship toward himself."[45] The prototype is the "self-made man," one who takes gifts and opportunities and exercises them in personal forms of attainment. The private self is the measure of all things—and it asks persistently, "How am I doing?" By contrast, the corporate self identifies with the other. Rather than featuring personal identity, it features identifying with the condition of the neighbor. While the private self seeks its own fulfillment, the corporate self strives for the fulfillment of the other and freedom from one's own needs and aspirations. The corporate is especially concerned with those who are oppressed and deprived. "To be freed is always a question of being enabled to identify with the *Marginals*, the people on the borders of society, through the power of the one (Christ) who started doing it."[46] The corporate self asks persistently, "How are they doing?" To be "born again" means to be free of the need to achieve one's own success so that one may participate in the process of fulfillment in the neighbor.

While American civil religion obviously nurtures public piety, it collates with individual initiatives driving toward personal achievement and success. We have already noted its frail capacity to mediate the prophetic dimension of the biblical faith from which would follow a concern for the marginals. In the absence of that sturdy and demanding theme, the provision of a context for personal fulfillment becomes controlling. The sense that one can always better oneself and one's own condition is pervasive in public piety and remains uncontested by American civil religion. The task of public policy ought to be to interfere as infrequently as possible in the journey of the private self and its quest for fulfillment. The sense of what is great about America is associated with personal freedom, and that becomes a euphemism for "benign neglect." The American way is one of opportunity accessible to all who are motivated to possess it. "The land of the free and the home of the brave" suggests a premium upon the individual and his capacities. The purpose of the nation is in the provision of an environment in which individuals can glory in self-fulfillment.

What is finally significant is that American civil religion does not seem to make systemic moves to free human beings from encapsulation by institutions. It has no sense of the dehumanization embedded in structures it sanctions. The flowering of the private self occurs naturally in the measure human striving is enacted. American civil religion fosters a nation of individuals and individualism; that, alas, leaves self-identity in control and identifying with the other unattended. The private self remains the reference point and human consciousness the point of impact.

Liberation theology aspires to engender the corporate self. It proceeds from the condition of oppression; the full force of human misery controls the theology and makes claims for recognition upon its themes. Liberation theology leads away from public piety and into a public faith because of its focus upon the corporate self. Liberation theology concerns itself with those who are getting hurt and with the systems and institutions that cause oppression. Personal fulfillment and achievement are peripheral; the self is not a primary reference point. The experience from which the theology comes is that of the marginal ones; that can only occur because one is born into a new consciousness. There is a death to self and a resurrection to the neighbor in need.

Freedom for identification rather than self-preservation is the goal; transformation of the existing order is the task. The difference between an alliance with the private self and one with the corporate self makes for different stories. They create disparate versions of the Christian faith. Perhaps the word *conversion* can be seen as the pivot point. The thrust of American civil religion links with a privatized faith, and conversion then collates with personal salvation. Being saved is a function of an individual's experience of Jesus. It is interesting to note the response of Billy Graham when asked why, as Richard Nixon's White House minister, he had not addressed with the president the issues of civil rights, Vietnam, and Watergate. Mr. Graham responded that he was a New Testament evangelist, not an Old Testament prophet; his task was to save individuals, not protest injustices. The evangelist is in many ways the high priest of American civil religion. Preoccupation with the private self and its salvation immunizes one against anything other than the status of another private self. There is a level at which the liberation theologian is not concerned with personal salvation: that is in the orbit of "How am I doing?" while the important question is "How are they doing?" because the "wretched of the earth" have priority. Being born again means being sufficiently free of self to identify with those at the margin of society. The difference is finally the dominance of a story of personal salvation or one of social transformation, finding Christ for oneself by oneself or finding Christ in the misery of the oppressed.

On the surface, American civil religion and liberation theology may appear to converge on the theme of a journey toward freedom—living in, living above, and living against one's circumstances. But the journey does not follow the same course and the ideas of freedom are not the same. American civil religion begins in the formation of an ideal for the nation, engages religion for the integration of society, and centers on the private self and its achievements. Liberation theology begins in the context of human misery, advances religion as the means of critique of a society that allows such misery, and centers on being converted to a corporate self. The overlap is in the code words. Civil religion enables us to live in our circumstances; liberation theology calls us to live above and against them as well. With its biblically formed vision of what ought to be, liberation theology sets the agenda for all forms of social transformation.

Notes

1. Robert Bellah in *American Civil Religion,* edited by Russell E. Richey and Donald G. Jones (New York: Harper Forum Books, 1974), p. 22.
2. M. Darrol Bryant, "Beyond Messianism," *Church and Society,* September/October 1973, p. 29.
3. Emile Durkheim, *The Elementary Forms of the Religious Life* (New York: Macmillan Co., 1915), p. 469.
4. Ibid., p. 469.
5. Andrew M. Greeley, "Civil Religion and Ethnic America," *Worldview,* February 1973, p. 21.
6. Peter Berger, *The Sacred Canopy* (Garden City, N.Y.: Doubleday Anchor Books, 1969), p. 19.
7. Ibid., p. 28.
8. Ibid., p. 25.
9. Richey and Jones, *American Civil Religion,* p. 15.
10. Will Herberg, "America's Civil Religion" in Richey and Jones, *American Civil Religion,* p. 78.
11. Charles P. Henderson, *The Nixon Theology* (New York: Harper and Row, 1972), p. 193.
12. Robert Jewett, *The Captain America Complex* (Philadelphia: Westminster Press, 1973), p. 33.
13. Martin Marty, "Two Kinds of Two Kinds of Civil Religion," in Richey and Jones, *American Civil Religion,* p. 145.
14. Robert Bellah, "American Civil Religion in the 70's," in Richey and Jones, *American Civil Religion,* p. 256.
15. Robert Bellah, "Civil Religion in America," in Richey and Jones, *American Civil Religion,* p. 40.
16. Ibid., p. 40.
17. Ibid., p. 21.

18. Robert N. Bellah, *The Broken Covenant* (New York: Seabury Press, 1975), p. 14.

19. Robert Bellah, "The Revolution and Civil Religion," in *Religion and the American Revolution*, Jerald C. Brauer et al. (Philadelphia: Fortress Press, 1976), p. 56.

20. Ibid., p. 57.

21. Ibid., p. 73.

22. Bellah, *The Broken Covenant*, p. 12.

23. Richard Neuhaus, *Time toward Home*, (New York: Seabury Press, 1975), p. 196.

24. John N. Wilson, "An Historian's Approach to Civil Religion," in Richey and Jones, *American Civil Religion*, p. 121.

25. Wolfhart Pannenberg, *Theology and the Kingdom of God* (Philadelphia: Westminster, 1969), p. 125.

26. Herbert Richardson, "Civil Religion in Theological Perspective," in Richey & Jones, *American Civil Religion*, pp. 161–84. See also Bellah, in Richey and Jones, *American Civil Religion*, p. 258.

27. Jürgen Moltmann, "A Critical Political Theology of Christians and the Civil Religion of a Nation," unpublished paper, p. 6.

28. John Coleman, "Civil Religion and Liberation Theology in North America," *Theology in the Americas*, edited by Sergio Torres and John Eagleson (Maryknoll, N.Y.: Orbis Books, 1976).

29. Ibid., p. 114.

30. Ibid., p. 116.

31. Ibid., pp. 120–21.

32. Ibid., p. 126.

33. Ibid., p. 131.

34. Robert Bellah, "American Civil Religion in the 1970's," in Richey and Jones, *American Civil Religion*, p. 266.

35. Ibid., p. 263.

36. Enrique Dussel, *History and the Theology of Liberation* (Maryknoll, N.Y.: Orbis Books, 1976), p. 27.

37. Hugo Assmann, *Theology for a Nomad Church* (Maryknoll, N.Y.: Orbis Books, 1976), p. 104.

38. Quoted from Dussel in Alfredo Fierro, *The Militant Gospel* (Maryknoll, N.Y.: Orbis Books, 1977), p. 210.

39. Michael Harrington, *The Vast Majority* (New York: Simon and Schuster, 1977), p. 34.

40. Richard Neuhaus, *Time toward Home*, p. 201.

41. Moltmann, "A Critical Political Theology of Christians and the Civil Religion of a Nation," p. 3.

42. "Preparation Document no. 2, Guidelines for Reflection Group," in *Theology in the Americas*, edited by Sergio Torres and John Eagleson, (Maryknoll, N.Y.: Orbis Books, 1976), p. 17.

43. Peter Berger, *A Rumor of Angels* (Garden City, N.Y.: Doubleday, 1969), p. 7.

44. Frederick Herzog, *Liberation Theology* (New York: Seabury Press, 1972), pp. 14–15.

45. Ibid., p. 63.

46. Ibid., p. 64.

4 Stories Economists Tell

American civil religion uses biblical imagery to symbolize the American experience. Because it draws its assumptions from within the existing system, it loses contact with the biblical faith and inevitably becomes an apologist for "what is." The prophetic sense of "what ought to be" is at best fragile since present conditions dominate future visions. Rather than being agenda setting for the social order, American civil religion collapses into a prop for the status quo. A similar phenomenon can be seen in the prevailing analysis of the American economic system. Economists, of course, use analytic models and not biblical imagery. However, "a model is a symbolic representation of selected aspects of the behaviour of a complex system for particular purposes. It is an imaginative tool for ordering experience, rather than a description of the real world."[1] Economic models are based on certain value premises about the nature of the society. The models explain the behavior of an economic system characterized by those values. For example, in the United States, private-property ownership is a basic value. Economic analysis accepts that and attempts to explain how a private-property system will perform economically. If the society believes in the economists' value premises, it will accept the models as descriptive of reality. The models can be used to make sense out of the American experience just as the biblical imagery of American civil religion is used for that purpose.

It has already been argued that stories are a narrative expression that allows intuitive understanding and transmission of values which support a given economic, social, political, or cultural system. Models are a representation of the structural components that make up such systems. In a sense, models are embryonic stories. Stories used to convey experience in the economic order grow out of a model of behavior thought to be identical with reality. When the society accepts the values that support the models as the ones which prevail in the society, they also believe the economists' stories. But, just as Veblen contended, the models can continue to hold sway and to dominate thought and behavior even after the basic economic conditions have changed. The value premises that are imbedded in the analysis may no longer apply, but the model lives on, providing a story that has lost contact with reality.

The continued dominance of these outmoded economic stories liquidates the tension between "what is" and "what ought to be." Because there is a prevailing belief that these economic models and their associated stories are describing reality, the economist becomes an apologist for the prevailing system. Like the proponents of American civil religion, economists find themselves engaged in an affirmation of the prevailing order and rarely assume the prophetic risk of calling the system into question and demanding an alternative future.

One of the tensions in our economic system is between the pursuit of self-interest and the welfare of the society at large. Economic analysts, drawing upon Adam Smith, claim that this tension is dissipated because the competitive market system will turn the individual's self-interested economic action to the good of society. This argument will be developed more fully later in this chapter, but at this point it can be seen how such a belief can act as an "ideological screen" to block out a broader vision of societal good. When the competitive conditions no longer exist, pursuit of self-interest leads to an undesirable outcome; acceptance of the model as a descriptive story can blind us to that outcome. Because the society in general does accept competitive economic models as valid descriptions of reality, it becomes unwilling to view acceptable economic actions as unacceptable in terms of society's goals.

American economists use models to explain the behavior of the American economic system. For the noneconomist, that often translates into "how to be financially successful." Many of the American stories discussed earlier celebrate economic success in business as being the preeminent goal of individuals. The economic models and their associated stories are used both to explain and to justify success in business. For some in the society, however, there is a real tension between the good of the individual or the corporation pursuing economic success and the good of the society at large. Eli Black, the former chief executive officer of United Brands, exemplifies the ways in which this tension can become unbearable.

United Brands is a conglomerate that includes the old United Fruit Company. Black was a brilliant business manager and organizer who made United extremely successful in economic terms. He was also a devout Jew who brought from that tradition a deep social conscience and a concern for the welfare of human beings. He fostered many innovations in United Fruit's Latin American activities, including higher pay, better living conditions, and improved health facilities for the plantation workers. "When Eli Black was advised by his colleagues at United Brands that the market conditions did not demand that he be so generous with the Latin American workers, he responded that in order to be true to his own convictions he had to be considerate of the welfare of these laborers."[2]

On February 3, 1975, Eli Black committed suicide. His company had recently turned the corner after a sticky six months due to unfavorable climatic conditions. He had also pulled off a major coup by selling one of his subsidiaries at a huge profit and generating substantial working capital. He was part of a warm and mutually loving family. What could have caused his suicide while at the height of his personal and corporate success? One speculation is particularly plausible. During the autumn of 1974, United Brands had paid a $2.5 million bribe to a Latin American official in return for reducing a new tax on bananas. Apparently Black knew about and approved the bribe. Such an action must have cut deeply into Black's moral convictions. Economic analysis would show the bribe as contributing significantly to business success; at the same time, it was a clear violation of his Judaic commitment to social responsibility. The tension created by this violation could well have been an important factor contributing to Black's suicide. He tried to live both the economic story of success in business and the religious story of concern for the social order. He discovered that these stories rested on conflicting values and his inability to reconcile them may have destroyed him.

To be sure, not everyone feels and experiences that tension. Indeed, much of the business success experienced by individuals and organizations within the economic history of the United States can be traced to intensive pursuit of economic self-interest without any concern for social welfare. The stories that are used to typify success in America are filled with such an untroubled vision. We will examine some of these before we explore the role that economic models and analysis have played in supporting this vision.

A. The American Success Story

The American story elevates the role, place, and achievement of the individual. To a degree true nowhere else, any typical American can make the system work and be rewarded with wealth, income, power, and status. This is particularly true in business, where men such as Andrew Carnegie, John D. Rockefeller, and Henry Ford started with little more than intelligence, ambition, and courage. By using these qualities to the fullest they became major industrialists and multimillionaires.

The waves of immigrants who came to this country were largely illiterate and poor. Equality of opportunity, an egalitarian educational system, and the indifference of the profit-and-loss mechanism of the market system enabled their children to move into the mainstream of American life. Many of them became wealthy. For them, the United States was truly the land of opportunity.

Andrew Carnegie is a typical American success story.[3] Born in Scotland in 1835, he emigrated to the United States in 1848. His first job in America was as a bobbin boy in a textile factory where he earned $1.20 per week. Carnegie quickly became a telegrapher's boy and then, in 1850, a telegraph operator, at which he earned $4.00 per week. His intelligence and ability greatly impressed Tom Scott, the superintendent of the western part of the Pennsylvania Railroad. Scott not only hired Carnegie as a secretary, but financed him in ventures that made Carnegie wealthy. In 1859, Carnegie succeeded Scott as western superintendent for the railroad, a position he held until 1865. In 1863, Carnegie, his brother Thomas, and some other friends became involved with the Kloman Brothers steel works. Now Carnegie's interests were very diversified; he had holdings in companies involving steel, wrought iron, bridge building, oil, telegraphy, and banking. By 1870, his annual income was more than $50,000.

In 1872, Carnegie decided to "put all of his eggs in one basket and watch the basket" by specializing in steel production. The next year, Carnegie, McCandless, & Company built a new steel works at Braddock, Pennsylvania. Mergers and reorganizations followed, with Carnegie's share always growing larger. The most significant merger came in the early 1880s when Henry Clay Frick's coke business was integrated into the Carnegie interests. This marked the beginning of the complete vertical integration that was the most significant innovation introduced by Carnegie.

In 1901, Carnegie retired. The Carnegie Company, Inc., was sold for $480 million to a combine headed by J. P. Morgan. The combine used the Carnegie interests as the bellwether of the newly formed United States Steel Corpo-

ration. It controlled about 60 percent of the American market.
Carnegie had the most successful steel company in the United States because of vertical integration and meticulous adherence to rigid cost-accounting procedures. Carnegie himself was a success because he worked hard, was innovative, and could foresee future markets and the benefits of careful cost reduction. In a competitive world, Andrew Carnegie was the competitor par excellence.
There are many other examples of American success stories. Joseph Kennedy amassed a fortune in the stock market, in real estate, and in the movie business. His parents were immigrants; he was a multimillionaire, and his son became the president of the United States. A. P. Giannini's parents were Italian immigrants, and he was able to go to school only until the age of twelve. In 1904, he founded the Bank of Italy, which was later to become the Bank of America—the largest commercial bank in the United States. Patricia Harris, the daughter of a black family in Mattoon, Illinois, became a member of a prestigious Washington law firm, a law school professor, and a dean. Active in Democratic politics for many years, she served as the United States ambassador to Luxembourg and as the first black woman Cabinet member. Babe Ruth was raised in a boys' home in Baltimore, Jim Thorpe on an Indian reservation, and Joe Louis as a sharecropper's son in Alabama. By using their talents to the fullest, each was able to win worldwide acclaim and receive significant status and rewards. Lyndon Johnson, born and raised in poverty-stricken conditions in Texas, was able to educate himself by hard work. After his law degree, a political baptism in the office of a Texas Congressman led to membership in Congress, leadership of the Senate, and finally, the presidency. These are stories that many Americans would hold as typical of the possibilities and opportunities in the United States.
The outgrowth of the dominance of individualism in these

American stories is the idea that anyone who really wants to can "make it" in America. A corollary is that those who fail do not want success enough. Failure is thus personal and individual. There is no excuse for poverty or unemployment except for those few who are physically or mentally handicapped and prevented from competing. Excluding that small group, those who work the hardest, compete the most effectively, and have the strongest desire for success will achieve it.

The historic possibilities for economic success in America rested upon the values inherent in the Puritan ethic, a philosophy of Social Darwinism, and a virtually unregulated business environment. The Puritan ethic contributed the twin values of hard work and personal restraint. The hard work enabled some to generate surpluses, while the personal restraint eschewed consumption in favor of the capital investment necessary for economic growth. Social Darwinism coated the sometimes rapacious behavior of entrepreneurs and capitalists with a veneer of acceptability by equating economic success with the natural evolutionary process of "the survival of the fittest." Andrew Carnegie drew heavily upon Social Darwinism as justification for his actions in building the Carnegie steel interests.[4] Finally, the absence of regulation allowed for vast individual and, particularly, corporate accumulations of power. This, in turn, fostered the observed economic and political successes of individuals.

The story of the land of opportunity does not just imply that anyone can get ahead economically or politically; it also signifies that anything is possible and that even the most ambitious dreams can come true. No matter how many leaps of imagination are necessary to move from the horse to the automobile to the airplane to a walk on the moon, all are possible because America has provided a climate that encourages individuals to achieve and places no limits on the rewards. This story is consistent with the sufficiency of the story of Sara and Abraham; "wild, irrational hope" can be fulfilled without transformations of the existing order.

B. The Neoclassical Story

When Western economists attempt to explain the behavior of capitalist or free-enterprise economic systems, the starting point is always the market. The benefits that such systems bestow upon their participants arise because the market is an efficient allocator of goods and services and of human and nonhuman resources. The basic assumptions are that individuals will pursue their own self-interest in all of their economic actions and that competition will exist in all markets. The competition will force the self-interested participants in the market to undertake actions that also serve the best interests of society. For example, an individual producer and seller of a product, trying to maximize profit for personal gain, will find that the only way to do that is to serve customers effectively. Failing that, some competitive producer will offer better service, and the customers will desert the first producer and move to the second. The first producer will make no profit at all. The existence of the competitive market allows the customers to choose among various producers and forces them to maintain the cost, quality, and service conditions that the consumers desire.

It is this vision of the economic system that serves as the basis for American success stories. The story extols the personal economic success of Andrew Carnegie because of an implicit assumption that it was achieved by faithfully serving the best interests of society. Carnegie became wealthy because he was producing effectively those goods and services which society needed. If he had failed to serve social interest, then he would have been forced into some other business or into bankruptcy. Because we want to believe in the success stories, it is an easy step from defining the conditions that would render them true to accepting those conditions as descriptive of reality. Because the conditions are significantly violated, a considerable part of the American economic system lies outside the competitive economic model. The positive outcomes associated with the operation of that model cannot be expected to be universally or even abundantly present within the United States. Nonetheless, the American success stories condition a belief in those positive outcomes and an acceptance of the system as an active promoter of individual and societal welfare. To support that contention, it is necessary to show how the system is supposed to work according to the competitive model and to demonstrate how the violation of certain basic assumptions vitiates the welfare-enhancing aspects of the model. The following argument is essentially intuitive. A formal graphical analysis is presented in the appendix at the end of this chapter.

Economists in the first half of the nineteenth century began turning to the market as *the* mechanism for allocating resources, determining income distributions, and maximizing societal welfare. Their bible was Adam Smith's *Wealth of Nations,* published in 1776, which argued that, if competitive forces were unleashed and allowed to flourish, society would be served well and efficiently. This was in sharp contrast to the prevailing economic philosophy of mercantilism that controlled the economic activity of the country through various licensing and monopoly grants from the government.

In the early nineteenth century the followers of Smith developed doctrines of economic behavior that came to be known as the classical school of economics. These doctrines were the cornerstone of free-trade, laissez-faire capitalism, which became the model for economic behavior and policy in both England and the United States. The analytic justification for the claims of the classical economists was first fully developed in the 1870s by Jevons, Menger, and Walras. These neoclassical economists discovered the marginal principle, and their organization of economic thinking and its later refinements by Marshall, Chamberlain, and Robinson are the subject of this section.

Smith's basic claim was that a nation is enriched by the productive efforts of its members. He searched for the proper way to maximize the impact of those productive efforts. Smith reasoned that using resources efficiently would maximize resource contributions. Competition was the force that guaranteed resource efficiency. For example, if labor was being used inefficiently by a business, costs would rise and prices would have to go up. Competing businesses that used labor efficiently would be able to sell their product at a lower price; the inefficient business would find itself with no customers. That had to be good for the society in terms of assuring the best possible resource use. Competition is the keynote of Smithian, classical, and neoclassical economic thinking.

During the last third of the nineteenth century, the neoclassical economists made clear *how* the competitive forces operated to achieve efficiency and societal welfare by pursuing self-interest. The paradigm for their analytic purposes was perfect competition. Such competition was characterized by a large number of buyers and sellers of a homogeneous product. No single buyer or seller could significantly influence the market price of the product. Each person or firm in the market had perfect information about market conditions. Each knew how others would respond in a given situation. Finally, there must be no barriers preventing new producers from entering the industry or market. These conditions were necessary in both the markets for goods and services and in the markets for factors of production—labor, land, capital, and managerial ability.

Under neoclassical assumptions and analyses, a typical household has only labor services to sell in the factor markets. As a reward for the contribution of labor services, the family receives an income which it uses to buy various products. The household has a choice between work and leisure. Work brings in income that provides for consumption, but it decreases the leisure time available to enjoy that consumption. The household seeks to maximize its satis-faction from the joint use of income and leisure time.

The household's labor is used to produce goods and ser-vices. The typical business firm hires labor and other re-sources and sells products to consumers. Its goal is to max-imize profit by using resources as efficiently as possible to produce the goods and services consumers desire. Eco-nomic profit means that a firm is able to cover all of its costs, including a normal rate of return on the capital em-ployed in the business and a salary for the entrepreneur, and still have something left over. For example, if an entre-preneur could get a 10 percent return by using capital to purchase certificates of deposit, then a production activity must provide at least a 10 percent return. In such a case, it is only after the rate of return rises above 10 percent that there is an economic profit.

Profit acts as a signal to tell firms in an industry whether or not they are using resources properly. If a firm is making economic profit, that is a sign to it (and to competing firms) that more resources should be devoted to the production of that product. As more of a product comes on the market, the price falls, which reduces or eliminates the economic profit. If there is economic loss, too many resources are being used in the industry and some firms should leave. The free movement of firms into and out of a competitive indus-try will ensure that in the long run all firms make only a normal rate of return, none makes an economic profit. In order to make even a normal return in the long run, all firms will be forced by competitive pressures to respond to the dictates of consumers and produce those goods consumers demand at the lowest cost. This is the reason why such a system serves to maximize the economic welfare of soci-ety.

The argument of the competitive neoclassical model is not just that self-interested economic behavior can serve the society's welfare, but that it will always so serve. Obvi-ously, households and business firms make different deci-sions, guided by somewhat different principles; those different decisions must be congruent if society is to be served properly. Suppose, for example, that households make a certain set of work-leisure decisions, and that the resulting labor input is not sufficient to allow producers to manufacture enough goods to satisfy consumer demand. There must be some force that will operate to bring all of the decisions into line.

In such a case, the market for goods will be faced with excess demand (too few goods available). That will cause the price of goods to rise and correspondingly, the profits of producers to rise. The profits will act as a signal to produce more, but households will not supply any more labor services under existing conditions. Producers eager to earn more profit must induce a greater supply of labor services by raising wage rates. That causes households to change their work-leisure tradeoff in favor of more work. Therefore, the mismatch between supply and demand caused by incongruent household and producer choices is adjusted by the competitive market mechanism. Since all decision makers are now satisfied with the results, society's economic welfare is maximized.

The neoclassical economists were not just ivory-tower analysts; they were also perceptive policymakers. They recognized that perfect competition did not always prevail. There were indeed conditions under which, for whatever reasons, individual participants in the economic system did have enough size and economic power to control all or some part of a market. Under such conditions, the benefits of competition would not accrue. Marshall developed the general theory of monopoly in the 1890s, and Chamberlain and Robinson explored monopolistic competition and oligopoly in the 1930s.

Marshall showed how a monopoly firm, pursuing its self-interested goal of profit maximization, restricts output and raises prices relative to the behavior of a perfectly competitive firm.[5] The monopolist's control over the market enables it to sacrifice economic efficiency in order to gain more profit. Obviously, sacrificing economic efficiency reduces the overall welfare of society. The usual argument is that monopoly firms devote too few resources to the production of a good and therefore consumers get less than they would be able to get in a competitive situation.

The same thing is true in the markets for productive resources. For example, individual pursuit of self-interest in the labor market results in an appropriate set of work-leisure choices only if the labor market is a competitive one. If one firm or industry controls the market for labor in a particular locale, then they set wage rates and hours of work, leaving the individual laborer only with the decision to work or not to work. That is, the marginal decisions about working more or fewer hours are not open to the laborer. Under such circumstances, the automatic adjustment processes break down and the society does not necessarily have an appropriate set of choices. The individual worker, for example, could be faced with a choice between not working at all or working too much; neither is a welfare-maximizing choice. The existence of the monopoly power limits choice and therefore reduces societal welfare.

Robinson and Chamberlain extended Marshall's analysis.[6] Just as the world is not totally characterized by perfect competition, neither is it totally a world of monopoly. In between these two extremes there is a monopolistic competition and oligopoly. Few markets are completely competitive or monopolistic; most are in between, some more competitive, some more monopolistic. For example, corner gas stations are reasonably competitive, but customer loyalty and brand identification give them a small amount of monopoly power. Major automobile firms are very large relative to their markets, but the existence of three or four firms ensures some limited competition. All such firms share one common characteristic according to the neoclassical analysis: their pursuit of maximum profit leads them all to behave like monopolists—they restrict output and raise prices, which causes a reduction in societal welfare.

Despite these alternative models, two factors allowed the competitive neoclassical model to remain as the exemplar of economic behavior. Economists argued that markets were the most efficient way to allocate resources and products and that the force of the market pushed the system toward competitive behavior. In addition, the extremely rapid industrialization and growth in the United States and England occurred at a time when the competitive model was the only accepted model of economic behavior. All noncompetitive behavior was considered to be an aberration that would go away if only a true laissez-faire condition would prevail. The later theoretical developments that might have at least modified the prevailing economic story in the United States were swept away by the aura of success that surrounded the "land of opportunity." The field was left then to the competitive neoclassical economic model, and it became the foundation stone for most of the economic success stories. Who would want to abandon an economic version of the world that takes even our most selfish economic actions and converts them to the service of society?

Imperfect competition, particularly oligopoly, is the economic market structure that most typically characterizes the American system. Large corporate firms sustaining market control through advertising, capital barriers to entry, and ownership of raw materials are the dominant form of economic organization in American industrial capitalism. Economic analysis provides models that are useful tools of analysis for these forms of market organization. Unfortunately, even though oligopolistic firms dominate the reality of American economics, the competitive model dominates the stories of economic success.

There is no doubt that an economic system which satisfies all of the assumptions of the neoclassical perfect competition paradigm would achieve economic welfare for the society, but it is only *because* a system satisfies those assumptions that the market works to achieve welfare. Unfortunately, our economic stories have been constructed around this paradigm, and that has led us to assign the benefits from a rigidly competitive model to a much less competitive world. The competitive model gives rise to a story that does not accurately mirror the reality of our world. However, that story *is* a way of interpreting facts and behavior and it is capable of giving meaning to a situation, evoking strong defense of itself, and fostering the development of values that positively reinforce the story. It leads to the creation of institutional structures oriented toward the maintenance and dominance of these values.

The competitive neoclassical story provides the economic support and legitimacy for the generalization of the individual success stories that are so much a part of the prevailing American economic ethic. The belief in the efficacy of the market together with the successes of individuals leads to the belief that such successes are the typical result of human initiative. This, in turn, makes it difficult to challenge the existing order over issues of economic power, income distribution, and social welfare. Maintenance of the status quo serves the interests of those who already have economic and political power along with social prestige and status.

If we think back to the lives of Eli Black and Andrew Carnegie, we can see two contrasting ways in which this theme is played out. Carnegie lived the neoclassical story completely. It was easy for him to justify virtually any action within the sphere of his business activities. Whatever he did was simply pursuit of economic self-interest, and that was what he was supposed to do. Whatever the outcome, his actions had to benefit the society at large because that is what the economic story tells us. Black was trying to live two different stories, one drawn from the same economic milieu as Carnegie's and a second drawn from his religious convictions and their social consequences. The outcomes in his economic world were at odds with the goals he set for himself within his other story.

Black, however, may be an exception. Most of those who have economic power in the society are immersed in the story that grows out of the competitive neoclassical model. As a result, they believe that their actions within the economic sphere are fully justified. A benign and disinterested economic system ensures that those actions will lead to the benefit of society. For example, the classical and neoclassical economists objected in large measure to any government intervention in the economic system. In their view, such intervention interfered with the smooth workings of a competitive economic structure. Since that structure ensured societal welfare, intervention could only diminish welfare. Many in our society today have accepted that argument without recognizing that the underlying assumption about the existence of a competitive world is invalid. The United States' economic system is decidedly oligopolistic and monopolistically competitive. It falls far short of the perfect competition paradigm. It is time, therefore, for us to reject the story that claims that pursuit of economic self-interest always benefits society. If the journey toward freedom is to continue, we must formulate new stories that help us to understand how our world is really structured and that enable us to live toward a new and alternative future.

C. Revolution and Adaptation: Marx and Keynes

The neoclassical economic system is not monolithic. Economic analysis and the associated economic models have indeed been flexible over the past century. Despite this flexibility, economists have rarely had the power to challenge the prevailing competitive economic story. Critics like Marx have called for revolutionary change; others such as Keynes have settled for adaptation. Most such challenges have only reinforced and strengthened the story. The Great Depression of the 1930s proffered the most significant opportunity to question the prevailing economic story, but criticisms have arisen at many points and over many issues.

One of the first perceptive critics of the classical model was Karl Marx. His understanding of the economic world was the classical one and, in fact, he believed that the capitalist economic system worked very well indeed. However, the ultimate failure of the system would come from long-term internal contradictions. Marx saw the system as being very effective at seeking profit and at accumulating wealth. Labor power was the source of its productivity. The flaw in the system lay in the fact that the drive for profit and accumulation would always, in the short run, lead entrepreneurs to replace labor with capital. For the individual entrepreneur there would be a short-term profit advantage in this substitution. In the long run, competition would force all other entrepreneurs to do the same. Aggregate labor input and aggregate productivity would be reduced as a consequence. As aggregate productivity declined, all profit would be squeezed out of the system. At the same time, there would be an ever-growing body of unemployed laborers. This was the source of the recurrent crises or depressions that afflicted the economies of the industrial countries. In the long run, the "reserve army of the unemployed" would become so discontented with their unemployment and the conditions of their lives that they would overthrow the capitalist owners who were exploiting them.[7]

The basic problem with the capitalist world, in Marx's view, was that the laboring class was the source of the productive power of the society while the ownership of the tools of production resided with the capitalist class. The owners of the tools were able to exploit labor and take away a significant part of labor's productivity in the form of profit. As long as this distinction between ownership class and laboring class existed, exploitation would exist. Further, the competitive forces would drive the system toward the ownership of more and more tools by the capitalist class, unemploying labor in the search for profit. Under such conditions, class warfare and the overthrow of the system were inevitable. This would bring an end to private ownership of the means of production. In Marx's words, "the expropriators would be expropriated."[8]

Remember that the competitive neoclassical model predicts an outcome in which societal welfare is maximized. Marx does not quarrel with that conclusion in a static short-term analysis. Rather, he contends that the long-term dynamics of the system are such that one class benefits at the expense of another; that is hardly the proper condition for maximizing overall societal welfare.

Marxists have built their own story of economic behavior on this Marxist model, but their predictions of an overthrow of the neoclassical system have not come to pass. Marx was imbued with the classical vision of the world and drew from it what he thought were logical conclusions. He failed to realize the adaptability of the prevailing story and system. The story was modified by the neoclassicists so that each contributor to the production process (laborer, tool owner, etc.), got a reward consistent with marginal contribution to production. Thus profit could no longer be considered an exploitation of the worker, but was a just return for the entrepreneur's productive efforts.

In addition, some systemic changes helped to alleviate the revolutionary pressure Marx had predicted. Labor began to organize and this movement led to increased wages, higher standards of living, and greater job security. That lessened the obvious disparity between the top and the bottom of the income distribution and reduced the pressures of class hatred. In addition, the higher wages paid to men allowed women to leave the labor market. Later, "social reforms" like female labor laws forced them out of the labor market. By the middle of the twentieth century, female labor-force participation in the industrial sector was relatively minor. This reduced the growth of the total industrial labor force and the pressure upon available jobs. In the United States the widespread immigration of slaves and of other poor laboring groups bled off a significant part of class hatred into racial and ethnic animosity.

If there was ever a time that had all the earmarks of Marx's final crisis, it was the Great Depression of the 1930s. In the United States, with its inadequate machinery for supplying social services, 25 percent unemployment strained the system to its breaking point. The end of the reign of capitalism appeared to be at hand. But the Marxist prediction of revolutionary change did not come about; the system and the neoclassical story survived.

The prevailing order faced enormous pressures brought on by massive long-term unemployment and negative economic growth during the Depression. The neoclassical notion of self-correcting competitive markets was tested and found wanting. Even with drastic reductions in wages, there was not enough demand to employ all labor. Existing analysis could not cope with problems of that scale. The system was floundering and seemed incapable of solving any of its own problems. In the midst of that, a new theoretical paradigm emerged which seemed to call for a fundamental change in analysis and policy but which actually became an adaptation of the neoclassical model to fit the new conditions.

In 1936, John Maynard Keynes published *The General Theory of Employment, Interest and Money,* a criticism of self-correction in the neoclassical model. For Keynes the failure of correction resulted from significant, noncompetitive elements in the labor market and long-term insufficient demand for goods and services.

Prior to Keynes, aggregate economic activity was traditionally viewed only as a consequence of the behavior of individual decision makers. Aggregate economics was inherently uninteresting; if the competitive forces were operating properly at the individual level, the aggregate system would always be at or tending toward full employment. Conditions of unemployment would be counteracted by competition among workers, which would force wages down and make labor a more attractive resource. For Adam Smith, the wealth of nations was maximized by maximizing the productive contributions of individuals. The latter was assured by encouraging competition and minimizing governmental interference. Keynes pointed out that less than optimal conditions could prevail and yet the system would not, by itself, correct the deficiencies. For example, large industrial corporations as buyers of labor and/or large labor unions as sellers of labor do not fit the picture of the perfectly competitive labor market. In fact, their relationship creates a condition in which the wage rate can not be reduced and the solution to unemployment described above will not occur.[9] In addition to the labor-market problem, Keynes showed that there can be insufficient demand in the system. While the process of production generates enough income to buy all of the goods produced, the income will *not* necessarily be used to buy them. Aggregate demand does not equal aggregate supply. The shortage of aggregate demand generates unemployment. In Keynes's view, no self-correcting mechanism existed to ensure a return to full employment.[10]

The Keynesian solution called for government policy actions to raise aggregate demand and stimulate employment. When the market failed to equilibrate aggregate demand and supply, there was a legitimate role for government intervention to achieve more desirable conditions. Such solutions were not supposed to supersede or supplant the market mechanisms, but rather to supplement them.

It is paradoxical that one of the consequences of this Keynesian critique is that the competitive neoclassical story was able to survive. Keynes viewed himself as challenging the economic orthodoxy, but his theories gave it new life. In the face of the massive economic discontent and outright failure throughout much of the industrial world during the 1930s, the Keynesian "revolution" modified and justified the continued existence of the prevailing economic order. This does not mean that diligent application of Keynesian principles pulled us out of the Depression; World War II is primarily responsible for the cure. Rather, the Keynesian revolution gave us new ways to explain old behavior so that the story of the competitive, market-responsive system could be maintained even in the face of the clear failures of neoclassical mechanisms.

Most economists regard the Keynesian analysis as a discovery of some new ideas and a reformulation of some old ones so that we could better understand the economic system we were examining. Galbraith contends, however, that the Keynesian analysis was more of an adaptation to change than a new discovery.[11] The objective conditions of the economic system had significantly changed because of the increasing dominance of large corporations and other economic institutions that were insulated from the market by their size and their monopoly power. The Keynesian analysis was picking up that change and casting it in a form that made it a logical extension of neoclassical market behavior rather than an aberration. It was relatively easy for the system and the institutions to adopt this Keynesian critique to serve their needs. Despite the neoclassical outcry against government intervention, many of the giant oligopoly corporations would find it difficult to survive without extensive government participation in the economy.

In the United States the prevailing economic analysis is broadly supportive of the market mechanism as *the* vehicle for allocating resources and distributing income. The economic story claims that all of the private sector's economic activities are subordinate to the market, prices are set by it, and profits are limited by it. The Keynesian subplot to this story allows us to treat occasional unemployment, slow growth, or inflation, not as a failure of the market system, but as an instance where government policy needs to be adjusted. Then the market mechanism can operate as it is supposed to.

In addition to this economic analysis, the competitive neoclassical story draws upon an economic value system that affirms in the most positive terms that the analysis is truly descriptive of the United States economy. In the midst of an energy crisis or an environmental crisis, the typical attitude is that the problem would be solved if we would just let the market function. The inflation of the 1970s was treated entirely as a problem of inappropriate government policy rather than as a result of the structure of the system. Big business and big labor are so insulated from the market that they have broad discretion over the level of prices and wages. It is this power which has been the most influential in extending inflation, not inappropriate government policy. As long as the competitive neoclassical model, the Keynesian addendum, and their associated values and stories dominate our vision, the existing system will be maintained; its faults and failures will continue to affect us. Even now, the neoclassical story, with this Keynesian adaptation, plays a dominant role in explaining away the revolutionary claims of neo-Marxists. During the 1970s, unemployment *and* excessive inflation were serious and chronic conditions in the United States. One is tempted to proclaim again that the Marxist ultimate crisis is upon us and the prevailing order is about to fall. However, our economic stories reassure us; our problems flow from inappropriate wage rates and public policy; the existing economic system is fundamentally sound.

This comforting belief is further reinforced by stories of individual success. In a Marxist world there would be no private ownership of the means of production; without that we could not have had an Andrew Carnegie, a Henry Ford, or a Joe Kennedy. Then where would we look for our vision of the world as it ought to be? Marxian analysis challenges the prevailing order that supports these stories; the Marxist story, therefore, must be wrong.

Obviously, the Marxist story is vulnerable. Labor is not the only productive element. The Marxian theory of value ignores other contributions. That leads to an analysis in which all profit is seen as an exploitation of labor. But the flawed theory of value should not be used to discount the validity of all Marxian analysis. The real problem is the accumulation of profit and the consequent expansion of economic power. Marx is clearly right about one point: acquisitive behavior in time creates disparity. The pursuit of self-interest does not provide benefits for all; it creates and serves vested interests. The promise of the competitive neoclassical economic story is dissipated in the reality of the economic system. Marx showed how, in the economic world, "what is" can be seriously out of sync with "what ought to be."

Marx and Keynes identified flaws in the neoclassical story. Keynesian analysis leads to adaptation; Marxian analysis leads to revolutionary change. Other critics assume positions between these two extremes.

D. The Persistence of the Neoclassical Story

The efficacy of the market for solving virtually all problems is gospel for most economists, businessmen, laborers, and consumers. Breaking away from the neoclassical story is extremely difficult. All of the rules for analysis and evaluation of economic phenomena have been formed from within the structure; an external perspective requires a wrenching effort.

Such an effort must be made if we are to evaluate in economic terms how well we are doing. We currently face the coexistence of relatively high levels of unemployment with rapid inflation. The availability of energy resources is a serious problem. There is extensive environmental deterioration, which can be traced directly to our economic and industrial growth. A significant portion of our population is living in poverty. Our cities are decaying physically and going bankrupt financially. Our educational system faces similar distress. Since these issues have dominant economic dimensions, we must ask why our market-oriented, private-enterprise, competitive system is not providing economic solutions to the problems.

The answer, of course, is that when one makes that wrenching effort to step outside of the competitive, neoclassical story, we all see that in many of these areas the market is operating poorly or not at all. There is serious doubt whether it *can* operate in those areas. Faced with the possibility of failure of the market mechanism, the neoclassical story begins to weaken its grip upon the psyche; alternative stories and associated structures become thinkable.

Criticisms of the neoclassical view abound, but most play out a theme of revision and reform. The critics are content to explain the sources of the flaws; they tell stories more in line with reality, but they resist calling for an end to the prevailing order. A new agenda demands recognition, but most economists have refused to respond.

Thorstein Veblen recognized the problems but did not provide a solution. He pointed out that all economic analyses rest upon largely unspecified assumptions about the nature of the institutional structures that define and delimit human life.[12] For example, the widespread support for the institution of private property in the United States has implications for our economic system, for the reward mechanisms we use, and for the relationships we sustain among the economic classes. Nonetheless, the existence of the institution of private property is itself taken as a given, and ensured by the weight and force of tradition. A second thrust of Veblen's analysis was that dominant institutions are constantly fighting a rearguard action to protect their vested interests from incursions.[13]

The most powerful economic force emerging in Veblen's time was the giant corporation. Its growth was spurred both by technological discovery and the agglomerating power of financial capitalism. This was the time of large firms; Rockefeller's Standard Oil and Carnegie's steel interests, among others, dominated their respective industries. The competitive world of the neoclassical economists was disappearing as the large corporation emerged. These corporations were controlled largely by the financial geniuses who put them together, not by the creative geniuses who had new product ideas. Access to dollars provided access to power. In Veblen's view, the overpowering role of the financial sector gave rise to a peculiar phenomenon of restricted economic output in pursuit of profit rather than a technologically expanded output in pursuit of societal welfare.[14] Monopoly power benefits the monopolizer, not the society. At the same time, the neoclassical model was being modified by Marshall and others to explain the nature of monopoly. This new analysis showed the economic logic of restricting output in order to maximize profit. As the model was modified, a corresponding institutional development was occurring. Antitrust laws and monopoly regulation were designed to return a semblance of market order to a situation that would otherwise have been insulated from the market. These corresponding developments allowed the society to remain comfortable with the competitive story because the story was covering up the changes that were really occurring.

Of course, the giant corporations already had begun to break away from market dependence and to control their own destinies through collusion, mergers, and advertising. As a result, they learned quickly to use all of the newly created regulatory agencies to their own advantage. For many years the Interstate Commerce Commission protected the railroads from competition. It certainly did not provide orderly competition within the railroad industry. Later, an amended Sherman Antitrust Act protected much of the corporate world from competition by supporting "fair-trade" laws. Until recently, the Civil Aeronautics Board provided the same kind of service for the airlines. Many economists contend that such regulatory activity has expanded the scope of monopoly power.[15] Under the cloak of the competitive neoclassical story, the assumption was that regulation was returning these monopolists to a marketlike condition. Once again, the story was used to protect the vital concerns of the vested interests.

Veblen was not taken in by this story. He recognized that the financial capitalists were the vested interests whose domains were being defended and protected by the system and the story. Since he believed in institutional evolution he saw the fight by these financiers as a rearguard action; the new wave of creative force by technocrats and engineers would eventually overwhelm the vested interests and a new era of productive plenty would emerge.

While Veblen was a perceptive critic of the system, he may have failed to heed his own message about vested interests. To a considerable degree, his predictions about the giant corporations have come true. Many of them have gone through a long period of technocratic domination. However, the problems of societal welfare have not been solved; we have simply been burdened with a new set of vested interests. The technocratic theme of expansion, supported by the discovery of new markets and the creation and extension of markets through advertising, has altered the problem. There are too many resources devoted to the goods and services produced by this technocratic structure, and not enough resources at work in the rest of the economy. Too much has been spent on oversized cars and not enough on clean air. The objective conditions of the economic system have changed, but the dominant story is still the neoclassical one. The story is still lulling us into a false sense of security; we are under the benign care of an impersonal market system which assures us that productivity will be rewarded and resources used efficiently—the consumer is king. This view of the world is no more true now in the days of the technocrat that it was in Veblen's time when financiers were the dominant force. Veblen's institutional analysis predicted changes in the economic system, but the revisions he foresaw did nothing to modify the accumulation of wealth and power in the hands of a few.

One consequence of technocratic ascendance was the demise of the owner as manager. It was no longer possible for one person to have effective control over the giant corporation. Such businesses increasingly turned to professional management teams to run their operations. The expertise required to make even relatively minor decisions dictated that decision making would become a group or committee activity. Since the owners were no longer able to understand the complex issues involved in decision making, they were at best relegated to prestigious but innocuous positions on the board of directors. But it was these owners, as operators and entrepreneurs, who had fueled the innovation that was the backbone of American industrial growth.

The perverse potential of this form of decision making

did not occur to Veblen, but it is the subject of extensive analysis by John Kenneth Galbraith. At the center of his criticism is a recognition that the increasing sophistication of technology forces organizational mechanisms to spread risk—both among more investors and through time. Large scale risk can no longer be undertaken at the behest of a single decision maker. The individual entrepreneur is replaced by a committee of specialists. They plan the future course of the giant corporation. They, rather than the individual entrepreneur, make investment, marketing, production and diversification decisions. Galbraith calls corporations whose size requires such group decision making the "planning system."[16]

Marx believed that this accumulation activity would ultimately lead to the collapse of the market system. Galbraith contends that the planning sector is *already* without a market structure. It is a part of the economic system where the market is an ineffective control mechanism. The market is gone, but the system remains. To be sure, this planning sector is representative of only about 50 percent of the American economic system. The rest Galbraith categorizes as the "market sector"; it still responds to market signals, strives to maximize profit, and has a very limited control over its markets. This market sector operates much closer to the dictates of the competitive neoclassical story and thus serves reasonably well the interests and well-being of the society.[17]

In Galbraith's view, the planning system operates largely outside the market. The prime interests of most corporate managers are the spreading of risk and the use of innovative technology to expand the size and scope of the firm. Their goal is no longer profit per se, but rather an expansion of the size of the firm so as to maintain their positions of power and increase their control. Sales maximization becomes a common objective. Since these firms are large relative to the markets in which they sell their goods and purchase their resources, the resulting monopoly power enables them to pursue sales maximization while maintaining a reasonable profit. The owners are ostensibly represented by the board of directors. The board lacks detailed expertise and is unable to judge whether profits are being maximized or not. They must be content with earning a rate of return sufficient to maintain the value of their investment. The managers, of course, must make enough profit to satisfy the owners and to ensure their ability to raise more capital when further expansion is desired. An example of management's power can be seen by the fact that even Chrysler Corporation did not have a major management reorganization in 1979–80.

In the perfect competition model, profit maximization ensures that resources are being used efficiently and consumers' needs are being met. In this new vision of the large corporate world, there is no such insurance. In fact, the firm may well create its own markets by stimulating consumer demand through advertising. Firms need no longer respond passively to market signals. Under these circumstances, it is difficult to support the notion that the market is operating; all of the arguments about market efficiency do not apply.

In all of this, the competitive neoclassical story plays a very prominent role in maintaining the position and power of the planning sector. As long as we believe that large business is subordinate to the dictates of the market, we will fail to take any corrective actions to alleviate the problems caused by the prevailing form of economic organization. Inaction, of course, enhances the power of the vested interests. Real regulation has always been an anathema to the American economic system; market efficiency and private ownership of the means of production have been glorified by the neoclassical story; interference has always been viewed as inefficient and destructive of societal welfare. This is a powerful deterrent to action.

Galbraith points out the negative impacts of large economic size and of bureaucratic structures, but he fails to push the arguments further. If these problems are a natural outgrowth of our economic system, then that system is fundamentally flawed and must be replaced. Galbraith attacks the system with fervor but finally calls for accommodation rather than revolution. He would have us face up to, live with, and control the planning apparatus forced on us by bureaucracy. That response does not answer the cries of human need that arise in our midst.

The spectrum of criticism runs from adaptation to revolution, and yet one common element is shared by all. The growth of scale and the creation of large economic organizations transfer the control of economic destiny from the individual to the system. That forces most in the society to live a divided existence; the neoclassical story elevates the role of the individual while the actual conditions continually subject the individual to the demands of the organization.

The stories and the reality of individual success would seem to be dramatically at odds with this critical view of our economic world. How have so many individuals made it in that world? It is tempting to answer by saying that all those individuals succeeded in spite of the system, not because of it. One can make a strong case for that view. For example, when a black woman like Patricia Harris rises to a position of power and prominence, that is a victory won against tremendous obstacles. It would also be unlikely for A. P. Giannini, the poor son of an Italian immigrant family, to become one of the most powerful bankers in America. In fact, all of the first-generation financial and political successes were achieved against long odds.

Rather than viewing these as victories in spite of the system, we ought to see them as victories desired by the system. The competitive neoclassical model and the stories built around it can survive and maintain their dominance if there are periodic examples of individual success in the society. The story makes us believe that the existing system is serving societal welfare; individuals who succeed reinforce that belief. As long as we believe in the ultimate dominance of the individual, then the large organizations that really hold the power are safe from our scrutiny. Whatever personal successes might occur then serve to reduce the discontent that might accrue among many groups in the society as a result of their disadvantaged conditions. We should not ask why Patricia Harris or Joe Louis made it; we should instead ask why so many blacks and women are permanently trapped at the bottom of the income distribution. We should not ask why some people, mostly white males, from poor and even immigrant backgrounds, were able to rise to the pinnacles of business, financial, or political success; rather, we should ask why so many are mired in poverty, malnutrition, and hopelessness. There is a difference between the success of one individual and the creation of conditions that ensure a decent life for all. "Wild, irrational hope" is *not* sufficient to free the marginals to rise above and live against their circumstances.

Appendix: The Neoclassical Model

The neoclassical economists carefully and rigorously developed a graphical construction of their reasoning. The effectiveness of their models, as well as the failures when the assumptions are violated, can be seen more clearly in the context of these graphs.

For an individual household, the desire for goods and services is considered to be unlimited, while the ability to purchase them is limited by available income. Assuming that a household has perfect knowledge of what is available, it must decide how to allocate its income. What particular goods and services should be bought and in what quantities? The goal of the household is seen as the maximization of satisfaction or utility derived from consumption. Utility increases at a decreasing rate as the quantity of a particular good increases. For example, one hamburger may bring ten units of utility, but a second hamburger adds only nine more units. The more we have the less we want more. Maximization is accomplished when spending is allocated so that no improvement in utility can occur by any other allocation of existing income. If we cannot improve, then we must be in the best situation possible under the given circumstances.

This consumer behavior gives rise to the typical market demand for a good that shows quantity desired as a function of price. As the price of a particular product rises, other things being equal, consumers will receive less utility per dollar spent on that good, and will, therefore, use less of it. For similar reasons, when price falls consumers will use more of a good. Price and desire move in the opposite direction. Household demand for the product is represented graphically in figure 1.

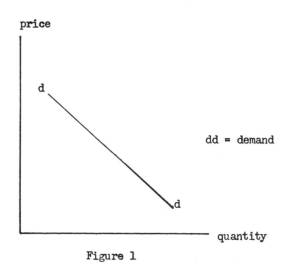

Figure 1

The next question, how much of the good will actually be available, is answered by all of the business firms that make the product. For the individual firm, the decision about how much to produce is related to the cost of production. That includes the average cost per unit of output *(AC)* and the marginal cost of producing one more unit of output *(MC)*. These are represented in figure 2. Average cost per unit of output at first declines as output grows, reflecting the ability to use factors of production more efficiently. For example, as more labor is added to the existing tools of production, the tools are used more effectively, and cost per unit of output declines. At some point the possibilities for such efficiencies are exhausted and output increases can be effected only with increasing cost per unit. Increasing average cost is reflected by the rising portion of the *AC* curves. Marginal cost is the additional cost engendered by producing one more unit of output. Typically, marginal cost will rise, indicating that the additional cost for producing output unit $n + 1$ will be greater than was the additional cost for producing unit n. In farming, for example, increased bushels per acre can be accomplished only by adding more expensive inputs such as machinery and fertilizer. This leads to a rising cost for obtaining additional output.

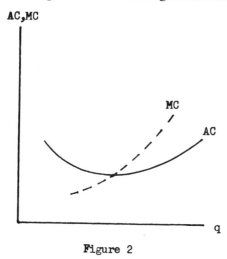

Figure 2

The firm seeks to maximize profit, which is the reward for engaging in the risk of production. If the firm can produce and sell one more unit and add to its profits, then it is not currently in a profit-maximizing position. If producing and selling one more unit adds as much to revenue as it adds to to cost, then there is no profit advantage to increasing output. A similar pair of arguments holds for decreases in output.

The change in cost for one additional unit of output has been identified as marginal cost *(MC)*. The addition to revenue from one more unit of output is marginal revenue *(MR)*. A profit maximum means that there is no profit advantage in changing output levels. According to the above analysis, that condition will occur when marginal revenue equals marginal cost *(MR = MC)*. Therefore, the individual competitive firm in making its decisions about how much to produce will find the output level where *MR = MC*. Given a certain marginal revenue, the supply decision is dictated by marginal cost, and the supply curve is an upward sloping function of cost and price (see figure 3).

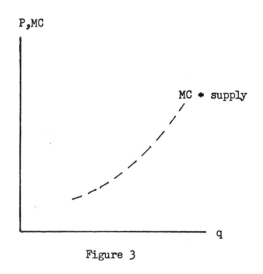

Figure 3

If we add the demand curves for all individuals, we get total demand for the product *(DD* in figure 4). Adding all supply curves yields total supply of the product *(SS* in figure 4). The sellers and buyers will compete with each other in the market and adjust their prices and quantities until the market comes to a resting place at point *E*. Here sellers can sell all they wish at price P_E and buyers can buy all they wish at that price.

Since all producers are small and no one individual can affect the market price, each producer is faced with price P_E as both the revenue per unit and as the marginal revenue from the sale of one more unit. That is, no matter how many units the firm sells, each one will sell at price P_E. The output decision must be adjusted so as to maximize profit in the face of P_E, a price over which the firm has no control. The desired output level occurs where $P_E = MR = MC$ (point F in figure 5). At this output level, q_F, revenue per unit, P_E, is greater than average cost per unit, q_FG.

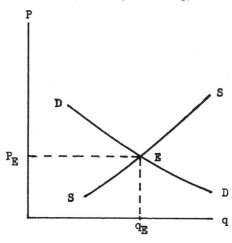

Figure 4

Thus there is an economic profit of GF per unit. If production rises by one unit, revenue will increase by P_E, but cost will increase by more than P_E; for all output levels greater than q_F, MC is greater than P_E. Increasing output will reduce profit. If production falls by one unit, revenue will fall by P_E, but cost will fall by something less than P_E; for all quantities less than q_F, MC is less than P_E. Once again, this will reduce profit. It is not profitable to vary output in either direction from point F.

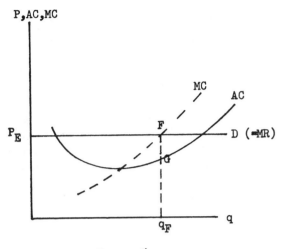

Figure 5

A short digression into the nature of economic profit is essential. The average cost curve represents all necessary costs. If $P = AC$, then the firm earns enough revenue so that it can pay all factors of production enough to keep those factors employed with the firm. This includes enough to pay stockholders or capital providers a return equal to what they would get if they put their capital to work in its next most productive use. If, for example, the market rate of interest is 10 percent, then capital providers must get at least a 10 percent return or they will pull their capital out and sell its services to some other firm. Economists call this return a "normal profit." The economic profit mentioned above is profit in addition to this necessary return covered by average cost. It is traceable to particular market and efficiency conditions facing this firm in the short run. As such, it is paid to the entrepreneurs, the organizers of the production activity, since it is their organization and willingness to accept risk that creates the profitable conditions.

Given perfect information and no barriers to entry, other entrepreneurs will know about the economic profit and will be encouraged to enter the industry and produce the prod-

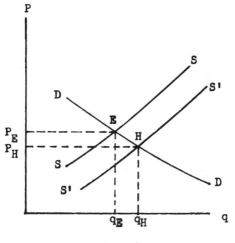

Figure 6

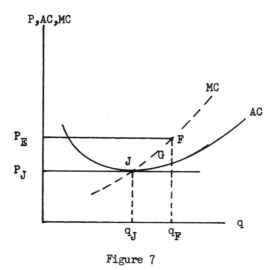

Figure 7

uct. If enough of them do so, they can, as a group, have an impact on market quantity and price; aggregate supply will be increased and the supply curve will shift from SS to $S'S'$, shown in figure 6. The result is a lower market price as P_E falls to P_H. This process will continue as long as there is economic profit to attract entrepreneurs to the industry. Ultimately, the price will fall to a level where no such profit is being made by any firm. This is illustrated by figure 7 by the combination of P_J and q_J.

In a competitive world all firms will be forced, in the long run, into a position similar to $P_J q_J$. Such a position is efficient and desirable for two reasons. First, the price, P_J, that consumers are willing to pay for one more unit of the good is equal to the marginal cost of producing that unit. Consumer willingness to pay matches up with the real resource cost of production. Consumer demand dictates where productive resources will be used. Second, all goods are being produced at the minimum cost per unit, which implies that all resources are being used efficiently. Thus the competitive system leads to a maximization of society's economic welfare—the system produces only those goods consumers desire and at a minimum cost. Any other configuration will reduce societal welfare either by producing goods in quantities consumers do not wish and/or by producing them inefficiently.

The institutions of profit and private property play pivotal roles in welfare maximization. The existence of economic profit in industry X is a signal that more resources should be devoted to production in that industry. The pursuit of profit will induce additional entrepreneurs to enter industry X and adjust the maldistribution of productive resources. Similarly, economic loss in industry Z is a signal that too many resources are being devoted to production in industry Z. Profit maximizing entrepreneurs will be forced to withdraw resources from Z to adjust the maldistribution. The private ownership of resources enables entrepreneurs to shift them readily into or out of a given industry as profit signals dictate. When the owner of a resource is an individual entrepreneur or an individual firm, the decision to shift resources is very simple. This ensures the maintenance and maximization of societal welfare; hence, private ownership and control are crucial to the effective functioning of the market system.

Competitive behavior in the goods market is echoed in the markets for resources and in production. Competition among laborers, for example, pushes the wage rate down to the minimum level consistent with the productive contribution of labor. The last worker hired produces output the value of which is equal to the wage rate. One's work pays for one's wages. If the firm stops short of the position where the last worker's productive contribution equals the wage rate, then the firm can add to its profit by hiring more workers. The value of the output produced by an additional worker will be greater than the cost (the wage rate) of hiring that worker. Thus, when the last worker's contribution equals the wage rate, the firm is using labor efficiently. Since all workers are interchangeable, they all receive the same wage rate. This is fair because it is appropriate compensation for the work performed. The worker's wages pay for the work. All factors of production are rewarded in the same way. The income distribution is determined solely by productive contributions, ensuring efficient allocation of productive resources and fair rewards for all factors.

This brings us back to the point where labor must decide how much productive service to offer and how much leisure time to retain at any given level of the wage rate. As long as competitive conditions exist in all markets and all decision makers weigh the advantages and disadvantages of adding one unit of income, or output, or labor input, the result will be system-wide efficiency in the allocation of resources, and the economic welfare of society will be maximized.

This analysis fits a perfect world, one that satisfies all of the assumptions underlying the perfect competition paradigm. The classical and neoclassical economists clearly recognized that there were some flaws in the world. Alfred Marshall explained the phenomenon of monopoly, which was the first analytic effort to understand an imperfect economic world.

The standard monopoly analysis deals with the "natural" monopolies such as public utilities. The capital costs of setting up a utility company are large, and the cost reduction benefits of expanding firm size are extensive. Therefore, it is sensible to have regional monopolies, i.e., only one electric company serving a given area. This is an "economies of scale" argument. It is grounded upon the notion that an average cost curve represents the average cost per unit of output for a firm of given size. A different sized firm will have a different average cost curve. For a natural monopoly, as the size of the firm increases, average cost curves move down, as in figure 8. While A and D both represent efficiency maximization points for their particular levels of output, D is a lower cost overall, and thus a more efficient point than A. Four firms of size A could produce the same output as one firm of size D, but the four firms would have average cost of P_A, while the one larger firm would have average cost of only P_D. It is cheaper to have

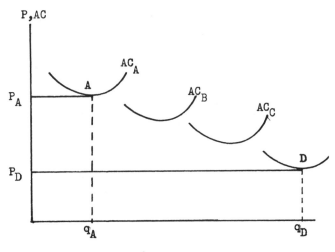

Figure 8

two thousand customers paying for one large generating plant than to have four groups of five hundred customers paying for four smaller generating plants.

Monopoly can also develop when some particular producer gains an advantage over competitors and earns economic profit. Such an advantage may be unrelated to costs. Instead of the competitive forces operating to eliminate the economic profit, the producer is able is able to protect that profit through some device like a license or a patent; alternatively, one may use the economic profit to buy up competitors. If this advantage over competitors can be maintained, the producer will eventually become large relative to the market. Large size allows the firm to influence the market and removes one of the assumptions that supports the perfect competition model.

Andrew Carnegie was in the forefront of effective cost control and vertical integration of the steelmaking process. By exploiting that advantage he was able to reduce competitive pressures in the industry and acquire monopoly power. The impetus for the creation of this monopoly power may be growth or market stability; it does not necessarily occur because of the existence of large economies of scale as in the case of utilities.

However monopoly power develops, economic analysis assumes that the basic goal of the firm is still profit maximization. In terms of the average and marginal costs of production, there is no conceptual difference between the monopoly firm and the competitive one. However, being in a monopoly position carries with it the ability to influence the market. Rather than accepting a price given by the market, the individual firm faces a typical downward sloping demand curve. The total market demand for the product is also the demand for the firm. When a competitive firm expands output by one unit it gains revenue equal to the unit price. Suppose a competitive firm were producing and selling 100 units of a product at $10 per unit. Total revenue would be $1,000. If they chose to increase output to 101 units, they could still sell each unit at $10, so total revenue would rise to $1,010. Marginal revenue would be $10 which is equal to the price of the product. Since a monopoly firm serves the complete market, it can sell more output only by reducing price per unit. Imagine a monopoly firm producing and selling 100 units at $10 each. Total revenue would be $1,000. Now, however, when the firm tries to increase output to 101 units, it finds it can sell that much only by reducing price to $9.95 per unit. Total revenue will rise to $1,004.95. Marginal revenue here is only $4.95, considerably less than the $9.95 price of the product.

Figure 9 shows the same result in a more general analytical way. At q_1 the firm sells its product at P_1 per unit, yielding revenue of P_1aq_10. When sales are expanded by one unit to q_2, market price per unit drops to P_2, and revenue becomes P_2bq_20. The market price must decline to induce the consumer to buy more. The firm gains some revenue, the crosshatched area cbq_2q_1. This is the additional unit sold multiplied by the new market price P_2. It is equivalent to the marginal revenue for a competitive firm. Due to the lower price per unit, however, the monopoly also loses

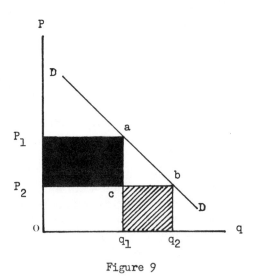

Figure 9

some revenue by expanding output. This loss is the shaded area P_1acP_2. The net revenue gained or lost by expanding output by one unit is the difference between the cross-hatched area (gain) and the shaded area (loss). This means that monopoly marginal revenue is less than competitive marginal revenue and price. Profit maximization always requires expansion of production until the gain from selling the last unit of output just matches the cost of producing the last unit ($MR = MC$).

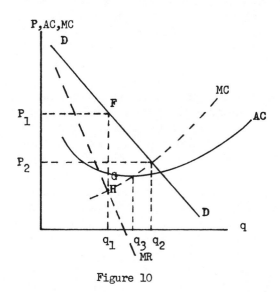

Figure 10

Figure 10 shows the impact of this analysis. The profit-maximizing monopoly operates at P_1q_1, the output level where $MC = MR$. A profit-maximizing competitive firm will operate at P_2q_2, the output level where $MC = P$. The first implication of this is that the monopoly firm will operate at a point to the left of q_3, the maximum efficiency position in terms of its cost curve. That is, it is profitable for the firm to restrict output and raise price even though such an action may reduce efficiency. The monopoly firm depicted in figure 10 is making economic profit of GF per unit. The monopoly power protects its position against encroachments by other firms seeking to exploit the profitability in this industry. The firm can keep others out and thus enjoy its monopoly profits indefinitely.

A related and more serious implication of monopoly is that the price consumers must pay for the product, P_1, is greater than the marginal resource cost of producing the good, q_1H. This means not enough resources are being devoted to the production of this good; consumers are getting less than they want; societal welfare, which depends upon efficient allocation of resources, is not being maximized. Unlike the competitive model, in the monopoly situation there is no self-correcting mechanism. The inefficiency remains.

A related issue arises with the development of "imperfect" or "monopolistic" competition. This occurs where there is more than one firm in an industry, but not enough firms to sustain the pure competition conditions. Through advertising, location, or quality differences in the products, each firm has some control over its markets and some monopoly power. In all cases of imperfect competition, the profit-maximizing firm will restrict output and raise price relative to the minimum point on the average cost curve. In the case of oligopoly, the firms are large, and each has a significant degree of market control. The steel industry and the automobile industry in the United States are prime examples. By reason of their strong market position and because of large capital barriers to entry, oligopoly firms are usually able to maintain their profit margins and earn economic profit in the long run. In other situations, smaller firms possessing only limited market control are subject to competitive pressures that will ultimately eliminate economic profit, but they will still restrict output and raise price. Neighborhood grocery stores and gasoline stations are prime examples. Imperfect competition, particularly oligopoly, is the economic structure that most typically characterizes the American system. Large corporate firms, sustaining market control largely through advertising, are the dominant form of economic organization in American industrial capitalism. Still, it is the competitive version of the neoclassical model that controls our vision of the economic world. In this version, the market, marginal decision making, competition, and profit maximization are the important mechanisms. In a truly competitive world, the model really would lead to optimal societal welfare since all resources would be used efficiently to produce goods and services in response to consumer demand. Furthermore, in the market for factors of production, the competitive pressures would create opportunities for individuals to succeed. The competitiveness of the market would allow superior talents, hard work, and drive to succeed, to be rewarded with status and income.

Notes

1. Ian G. Barbour, *Myths, Models, and Paradigms* (New York: Harper and Row, 1974), p. 6.
2. Oliver F. Williams and John W. Houck, *Full Value* (New York: Harper and Row, 1978), p. 145.
3. Herman E. Krooss and Charles Gilbert, *American Business History* (Englewood Cliffs, N.J.: Prentice-Hall, 1972), pp. 199–212.
4. Seymour E. Harris, *American Economic History* (New York: McGraw-Hill, 1961), p. 13.
5. Alfred Marshall, *Principles of Economics* (New York: Macmillan, 1920), Book V.
6. Joan Robinson, *Economics of Imperfect Competition* (New York: Macmillan, 1933); Edward H. Chamberlain, *Theory of Monopolistic Competition* (Cambridge, Mass.: Harvard Univ. Press, 1973).
7. Robert Lekachman, *A History of Economic Ideas* (New York: Harper and Row, 1959), pp. 211–25.
8. Karl Marx, *Capital* (New York: Modern Library, 1906), 1:837.
9. John Maynard Keynes, *The General Theory of Employment, Interest, and Money* (New York: Harcourt, Brace, 1936), pp. 4–11.
10. Ibid., pp. 280–91.
11. John Kenneth Galbraith, *Economics and the Public Purpose* (Boston: Houghton Mifflin, 1973), pp. 183–84.

12. Thorstein Veblen, *The Vested Interests and the Common Man* (New York: Viking Press, 1946), p. 4.

13. Ibid., p. 34.

14. Thorstein Veblen, *The Engineer and the Price System* (New York: Viking Press, 1954), pp. 36–37.

15. See, for example: Galbraith, *Economics and the Public Purpose;* or Walter Adams, "Public Policy in a Free Enterprise Economy," in Walter Adams, ed., *The Structure of American Industry,* 5th ed. (New York: Macmillan, 1977), pp. 482–514.

16. Galbraith, *Economics and the Public Purpose*, p. 44.

17. Ibid., pp. 44–46.

5   New Persons or a New Society

It happened on Broadway, Times Square to be exact. The hour was twelve on a hot summer night. The theater crowd was choking the street. One could hardly breathe. Then something happened—a youth with the face of a smiling idiot worked his way through the crowd, displaying the agility of a halfback and the determination of a fool. Frantically he waved a sign: "Christ for a troubled world." One had only to look around to know *how* troubled. Overhead was a picture of a sex goddess luring into the movie theater men who had nothing to give but their flesh; to the left was a woman much used of men shouting four-letter words at the faceless crowd; up ahead was a man without legs selling pencils to people in a fretful hurry to get nowhere important. And then that sign, "Christ for a troubled world." Christ seemed so pitifully helpless in the face of it.

A.   The Locus of Change

That incident raises the question of mediation: What is the means of passage from Christ to the troubled human condition? For the youth bearing the sign one can assume the answer lies in saving individuals from the world through a personal relationship to Jesus. If each could only know love and forgiveness, Times Square would be a different intersection. The sex goddess and street prostitute would be freed of their fleshly corruption; the cripple would be set to constructive tasks, perhaps within a community of faith. Christ saves persons *from* a troubled world. But the alter-

131

native is equally stark and direct. Each person is a victim in a social network. The sex goddess is the victim of a consumer system that violates personhood for profit, while the prostitute is caught in organized vice that may indeed link all the criminal elements in the city. The cripple may have learned to exploit his condition but he remains a victim of a society unwilling to care. Nothing short of a systemic revision can finally lead to freedom. Is the mediating principal personal transformation or the transformation of the social order? Which agenda is consistent with the Christian faith?

The options seem to be either to transform society by changing individuals or to change individuals by transforming society. The first is based on confidence that if one begins with love, justice will follow: the latter rests on the premise that if one begins with justice, love will follow. Being human in one's sphere or humanizing the sphere are the alternatives. Anecdotes count in both directions.It is not difficult to recall ways in which a changed individual made a difference in a system. But as a contrasting example, the 1954 Supreme Court ruling on educational segregation ultimately changed individuals through a revision of the social ground rules. Modern liberals move in with a swift affirmation of both, yet fail to provide a connection between the options. How are personal and social transformation interconnected? What is the relationship between the two stories of chapter 1? How do we enable persons to live in, above, and against their circumstances?

The economic issues in the preceding chapter are vexing examples of the need for mediation. If the neoclassical story is invoked, the man without legs selling pencils should have his meager earnings supplemented only by private generosity. Both the prostitute and the sex goddess should be commended for bringing a much wanted commodity to the market, but they must set aside something for the future when old age will make their product less desirable.

Of course, no one takes such an extreme view of the role and functioning of a market economy. As society has grown larger and more complex, it has also grown more impersonal. That impersonality has ruled out private charitable acts as the sole support of those unable to compete effectively within the market structure. Public welfare benefits have been substituted for private sector charity, but neither eliminates the factors that create the inability to cope with the system. Unfortunately, both treat the symptoms, not the disease. Similarly, blatant peddling of sex is exploitive of women who may be unable to compete effectively in more socially acceptable ways. Once again, the adjustments we make—whether in the form of anti-pornography, anti-prostitution laws, or in the form of pro-pornography and pro-prostitution laws—treat only the symptoms. They fail to deal with the underlying economic and social issues that create conditions under which some people can be only marginal contributors to the legitimate economic activity of society.

When we turn to the problems associated with oligopoly and monopoly power in large organizations, the mediation question becomes even more complex. Such organizations often use their power to protect their vested interests. Because of their size they are bound to have a profound effect upon individual members of the society and upon the general societal welfare. The neoclassical story, with its predominant role for the individual decision maker, argues that the reduction of that influence will be accomplished most effectively through the concerted actions of individuals in the market. To use an example relevant to energy, if automobile manufacturers are producing only cars with low fuel economy, people concerned about fuel economy should refuse to buy them. If enough people express their values in this way, it will reduce the profits of automobile producers—a signal to develop more efficient cars. While such an argument might be cogent in a competitive environment, it loses much of its strength once we recognize that the structure of these oligopoly industries helps to insulate them from the market. Thus they receive only imperfect signals and react imperfectly to those signals. The initial response to economic crisis in the automobile industry during 1979–80 led immediately to cries for protection from foreign imports, which disguised the need for the industry to respond to consumer and energy imperatives. Structural and systemic approaches are almost certainly mandated if real change is to be accomplished.

Why is it that we have a society in which individual initiatives for change are often so ineffective? How has a society founded on principles of individuality and individual achievement allowed the growth of a systemic structure that inhibits the role of the individual in bringing about change? How could a society that has the neoclassical story as one of its economic cornerstones evolve into a system in which prominent features of that story are negated?

The issue deepens with the realization that as persons produce society, society also produces persons. While on the surface these are contradictory claims, they "reflect the inherently dialectical character of the societal phenomenon."[1] Society would not exist without the action of humans, nor would humans exist in meaningful relation to each other and their environment without society. People form structures and then the structures shape people.

Peter Berger analyzes the process in its "inherently dialectic character" with a discussion of externalization, objectivation, and internalization.[2] Externalization rests on the contention that human beings differ from other mammals in that they are not complete organisms. We need finishing; we have a developing relationship to our own body and the world. There is a process of becoming that occurs as we express ourselves in our environment. A "continuous outpouring of himself into the world in which he finds himself" is essential.[3] Individuals develop a personality and appropriate a culture. While the world of the animal is closed, that of human beings is open. We fashion rather than adapt to what is given. The world, in a measure, is of our making. Unable to rest in ourselves and live self-enclosed, we express ourselves in externalizing action. While this world constitutes a culture in the largest sense, what concerns us is more narrowly a society. "Society is constituted and maintained by acting human beings. It has no being, no reality, apart from this activity."[4] Thus, society is a product of human externalizing. Objectivation occurs when the world we produce becomes an externalized product. It is distinct from its origin and takes on a life of its own over and against its creator. Society begins in our need to finish ourselves but "the humanly produced world attains the character of objective reality."[5] In the material realm it is obvious how what one produces exists outside of oneself: a person may produce a work of art as self-expression but it has a reality of its own once produced. This is equally true of the nonmaterial realm. One may create a value and be responsible for its existence in a social context, but soon it is a reality that affects its creator in the form of expectations or guilt. Thus the very society we produce "confronts man as external, subjectively opaque and coercive facticity."[6] It has the capacity to impose itself upon its point of origin. We are formed by what we form.

Internalization is the process of reabsorption. What is our own becomes internalized. That which has been objectivated finds its correlate in our consciousness, and we accept the objectivity of what we have created. Objective reality ceases to be only external. Meanings, for example, become once again *our* meanings through internalization. A new symmetry occurs. "Internalization, then, implies that the objective facticity of the social world becomes a subjective facticity as well. The individual encounters the institutions as *data* of the objective world outside himself, but they are now *data* of his own consciousness as well."[7] That ordering of experience which occurs through this world construction is recognized as having been produced by the human species and therefore integral to its sanity.

Berger's argument is that humankind inhabits a society that is independent of us even though it is a creation of ours: society depends finally upon human consent but human beings are under its jurisdiction as well. Society has a precarious existence because it depends on human consent;

the individual has a precarious existence because of dependence on society, without which chaos reigns. The consequence of this analysis for our concern is that any separation of selfhood and society is artificial; one takes hold of both in the grasp of either of them. The transformation of the individual inevitably has consequences in society; the reverse is also valid. The actualization of freedom cannot occur without transformation of the individual, but paradoxically, the actualization of freedom is contingent upon the systems of society.

B. Change in the Economic Sphere

Berger's analysis is evident in our own cultural stories and in their economic foundation, the competitive neoclassical story. It has already been suggested that the cultural stories grow out of a personal or individual vision that led many to see the United States as a cornucopia whose benefits are available to all willing to work diligently. The frontier legend reflects this and can be recast into Berger's terminology.

If the early colonists viewed themselves as living on a frontier that promised large rewards for those willing to take the chance, then it is easy to see how that personal value set became externalized into a societal value set. The objectivation process occurred as these early settlers came into contact with the seemingly limitless frontier. It is a logical outgrowth of that experience for people to begin viewing the United States as a place where infinite expansion was possible, where fortunes could be made and great status obtained by anyone bold enough to seize the opportunity. People at least thought they were casting off a more formal social structure where status was obtained by birth rather than ability. A new social system emerged in which people saw the individual occupying the dominant position.

As the society formalizes the prominent role of the individual, individuals begin to internalize that formal role and to view their own, and each person's, success or failure in terms of personal effort and talent. They begin to accept the stories in circulation. This negates the view that argues that at least some of the successes were due to factors in addition to the personal ones. For example, some of the frontier successes during the westward expansion of the United States may well be traced to better land or fortuitous location rather than to individual ability. While some of those circumstances may reflect an ability to recognize superior alternatives, many of them must be attributed to luck, or to advantages such as an inheritance that enables a person to buy the prime farmland or the best business location. But, in our traditional view of our own development, success accrues to the perceptive individual with talent and ability who works hard to overcome obstacles.

If this description is a reasonable one, the society formed from the individual-frontier interaction will be one in which achievement is perceived as an individual phenomenon. When the expected rewards from individual achievement are high, McClelland's n achievement factor will inevitably develop. The relationship between that factor and actual societal achievement has been demonstrated by McClelland and discussed in chapter 2.

Finally, it should be apparent that the American belief in the probability of individual success may play a very real role in its ultimate achievement. That does not mean the story makes us successful, but one can argue that the dominant societal values grow out of the same environment as the story. The story is a very important instrument for passing on those values. Widespread acceptance of the descriptive power of the story represents an implicit acceptance of that value system.

Any story that represents a set of societal values in a reasonably complex society must have some economic elements within it. In the case of the United States, the prevailing economic story is the competitive neoclassical one. It reinforces the individual success stories, the frontier stories, and the land-of-opportunity stories by providing a clear economic rationale for the individual success and economic expansion that have occurred throughout American history.

The competitive model imbedded in the neoclassical economic system is one where the signals given by the price and profit mechanisms will indicate to the individual where more intensive economic activity will pay off. Thus the individual—as an entrepreneur, an owner, a manager, or a laborer—can rely on the information provided by the market to make the decisions about where and how to use the productive resources he brings to the marketplace. Those who interpret the information correctly and make the best decisions will be rewarded. The individual does have economic well-being under personal control. As described in chapter 4, the competitive process is such that excessive profit accruing to one firm or entrepreneur will attract others to that particular business. The consequent increase in the supply of goods will drive prices down to a level where economic profit is eliminated. Thus the competitive process prevents the individual from achieving such an excessive accumulation that there emerges an advantage unrelated to ability. This natural limitation on accumulation also prevents the individual from being able to give excessive advantage to his children through inheritance.

One consequence of the neoclassical story is that individuals see themselves as having opportunity equivalent to that of others. Since all have reasonably equal possibilities, the system itself is then seen as benign, disinterested, and unbiased. There is little pressure under such circumstances for substantive modification of the structure.

The reality, of course, is that the system is not nearly so responsive to the needs, abilities, and efforts of all individuals. The rise of monopoly power has resulted in the exclusion of many groups from full participation in the system for reasons of prejudice and social or ethnic hatred. The lack of effective competition meant that these groups have had no lever with which to force their way into full participation in the system.

The pattern of American economic development has led inexorably to accumulation and to the creation of the giant corporations. Perhaps just as inexorably, it has led to the massive growth in the government bureaucracy that provides institutional support for the system. The labor movement might have been an effective counterfoil to this corporate and government growth, but instead the major unions often support the same basic goals as the corporations. This bureaucratic growth has caused and been caused by the expansion of monopoly power and reduced competitiveness. That, however, is only one of the reasons our economic system is open to criticism. A more crucial issue is that the growth of monopoly power and bureaucratic structures has encouraged the systematic exclusion of certain groups from the mainstream of economic and social life. The overarching value systems inherited from Europe and augmented by the frontier ethic in the United States have included widespread discrimination against nonwhites, non-Europeans, and nonmales. Our own Constitution, supposedly a model for democratic societies, initially counted blacks as only three-fifths of a person, accorded strong bias toward property owners in granting voting rights, and failed to include women in any serious role in the political structure of the society. A competitive economic structure would have helped to wipe out these discriminatory features—competition rewards productivity, not skin color or sex—but, with the increasing dominance of monopoly power and bureaucratic structures in the last half of the nineteenth century, these value systems were continually and effectively reinforced. No competitive pressures forced managers to hire blacks, even though blacks were a cheaper source of labor. By the beginning of the twentieth century, these patterns of discrimination in the economic sphere had been so completely institutionalized that they no longer required the willing cooperation of management. Large industrial corporations did not hire blacks because the long-standing pattern of discrimination against blacks had left them with poorer educations and lower levels of skills than their white counterparts. Indeed, they *could not* compete in the increasingly monopolized labor market. Women, too, found themselves in a position where the structure of the educational system and the sexual socialization process left them unable to effectively compete for many of the jobs in the industrial society.

The failure of women, blacks, and other minority groups to secure jobs in an industrial world that was becoming more and more dependent on capital and technology further increased the skill and income gaps between those groups and white males. In turn, and particularly for the minorities, the income gap meant greater difficulty in gaining access to quality education. In effect, a vicious circle of poverty formed, and it entrapped a very significant segment of the American population. Minorities and women were unable to do anything about their own situation. It is important to note that these conditions continue to prevail. Affirmative action and compensatory hiring have not resulted from changes within the economic system, but were forced by external political action. In the case of blacks, that political action has included both violence and passive resistance.

The pattern of discrimination against women, blacks, American Indians, Spanish Americans, and other minorities has had a devastating impact. These groups have had restricted opportunities and economic choices along with reduced economic status. They have not been able to exercise the full scope of their talents, skills, and abilities. Attitudes that denigrate the achievements of women and minorities have been inculcated in the members of these groups and in mainstream white males. Most of this damage has been accomplished by the establishment of economic, legal, and political barriers. These formal structures have institutionalized widespread societal values.

The existence of such patterns, of course, does not argue either for or against the role of the individual in bringing about change. We already know that the society has problems and that some of them, at least, are systemic in nature. The issue is, what is the proper approach to their alleviation? There are many examples in which individuals have had a profound impact upon the system, either for good or ill. With the publication of *Uncle Tom's Cabin,* Harriet Beecher Stowe became an important catalyst for the abolition movement; certainly, she had an impact upon the eventual emancipation of the slaves. Joseph McCarthy was a relatively obscure senator from Wisconsin when he began his probes into the alleged Communist connections of a number of prominent American political, military, and artistic figures. He had a profound impact upon the shape of American domestic and international politics during the 1950s. Martin Luther King was a charismatic leader who was able to bring together several disparate factions of the civil rights movement into a cohesive whole that was very effective at desegregating a large part of the American South. Susan B. Anthony, as a suffragette and a tireless campaigner for women's rights, led a battle that culminated in the ratification of the Nineteenth Amendment to the Constitution in 1920. Wilbur Mills, chairman of the House Ways and Means Committee during most of the 1950s and 1960s, was able personally to shape the tax structure of the United States and effectively block the use of the tax structure as a means of redistributing income. Cesar Chavez has organized migrant farm workers in California and other states; standards of living have risen, health and sanitary conditions have improved, and contractual obligations for employers have been established.

Despite these and many other examples of effective individual action to change the system, it seems clear from the economic and social structure of the United States that the systemic forces are more powerful than the individual ones. While the issue has its most intense focus on women and minorities, it encompasses a wide spectrum of the society. The growth of monopoly power and bureaucratic decision-making inexorably reduces the potential impact of any individual upon the system. In a competitive system, a relatively small group of consumers is able, by shifting its purchase pattern, to effect a significant change in the pattern of production. The profit and loss signals generated by consumer shifts will lead entrepreneurs to transfer resources from one activity to another. Monopoly insulates its holders from such shifts and therefore greatly reduces the impact of consumers upon the production pattern.

This phenomenon can be clearly seen in terms of the extremely slow response of American manufacturers to demands for good fuel economy in American automobiles, in the widespread presence of cosmetic additives in processed foods, or in the quality and lack of diversity of television programming. The argument is not that consumers have no impact; producers must, after all, sell their products. Rather, the monopoly producer need not respond to the wide range of consumer tastes. Instead, a narrow band of maximum salability is the target, with a consequent reduction in product diversity and a narrowing of the range of product quality. Those consumers who do not find their needs satisfied by this system in effect have nowhere to turn since monopoly power prevents new entrants into the production sphere who might wish to serve these unsatisfied needs.

Even more important than the existence of monopoly power is the creation of large bureaucratic organizations. Chapter 4 briefly discussed Galbraith's view of the ascendancy of the managerial technocracy and the consequent growth of organization. There has been a symbiotic growth of the large private organization (the corporate bureaucracy) and the large public organization (the government bureaucracy). More recently we have seen the growth of the large labor organization (the union bureaucracy). All of these bureaucracies have an interest in the maintenance of their own existence and a fear of intrusion by the "nonexpert." The only way that one can become an "expert" is by joining the organization. Therefore, all such bureaucracies have a built-in protection against the input of the dissenting individual. They do not respond to individual input and decision making, but to a group dynamic with a natural interest in self-preservation that supports the status quo. To put it another way, the necessity for group decision making inherent in bureaucratic structures is not likely to lead to bold new directions in economic, political, or social policy. Returning for a moment to the problem of blacks within the economic structure, the bureaucratic environment is one in which possibilities for real change are limited. Individual business leaders and managers have attempted to exercise a social conscience and find a place for blacks in their organizations. Henry Ford II opened up many jobs in response to the anguished outcry of blacks in the 1967 Detroit riots. Such efforts have failed because the system has left so many blacks with limited skills and education. This relegates them to the lowest-rung jobs on the industrial ladder; the jobs have very limited upward potential and are the first to be phased out in a recession. In addition, union pressures have resisted such efforts to give "white" jobs to blacks by insisting upon strict adherence to seniority rules. All of this leaves blacks at the very bottom of the industrial world with almost no upward mobility. It is not primarily overt discrimination or racial hatred that keeps blacks in these positions. Rather, it is the system, with its concentration upon productivity, profit, corporate welfare, organization, union work rules, and similar structures that prevent real economic mobility. In such instances, the good intentions of individuals will not have much influence upon the systemic conditions that create the problems.

C. Jesus and Transformation

It is inevitable that the Christian community will want to view the issue of transformation through Jesus of Nazareth. In his ministry is priority given to conversion of the individual or to societal change? Or, is there evidence of both?

Jesus' ministry to persons is self-evident. Those who contend that personal transformation was consistently up front are supported by an appeal to his teachings, his miracles, and particular encounters with individuals. His responses seldom follow through to an explicit action against the social context. Any contention that he aspired to free people by the transformation of the systemic forces around them generally rests in subtleties. Jesus dealt with prostitutes, Mary for example, in a way that led to inner transformation. His response was one of acceptance, not an attack on the vicious cycles in society that would drive women to prostitution. There are a number of occasions in which Jesus reacted to an individual's desire for wealth, but that did not lead into an assault upon the prevailing economic forces in the environment. Several times Jesus responded to individual tax collectors in ways that changed their lives, but the process of tax collecting, the procedural corruption, went unattended. He did not go for the jugular in the system. The thrust of his intervention was in lives, not institutions. Those who repackage Jesus as a revolutionary do so without clear warrant in the New Testament records. Recognizing that Jesus did not focus upon social structure as determinative in the relation of self and society should not cause us to overlook the point that "in an indirect sense, the manner in which Jesus thought and acted *de facto* broke open and transformed the social structures of the world in which he lived."[8] Obviously, in the first century A.D. we are not dealing with advanced stages of social organization that would lend themselves to attack and transformation. Those times had traditions and institutions that affected individuals. In subtle, sometimes direct, ways Jesus dealt with them.

The most familiar examples are in the organization and practice of religion. Jesus' teachings and actions are not confined to the spiritual realm. Cultic practice and religious authority fall under scrutiny. Jesus challenges those who are so rigid and ritualized that they give priority to Sabbath laws in the face of human need. "He is angered by the hypocrisy of those who equate God's commands with human traditions (Matthew 15:1–20). He cites Isaiah to condemn merely external actions that do not come from the heart, and he explicitly urges people to go beyond ritualism and legalism. He attacks those who claim to hold the keys to the kingdom but refuse entrance to others (Luke 11:52)."⁹ These words and deeds reach beyond the personal and into the public domain. On the surface they may appear to be confined to an attack upon the priestly class and, therefore, an intramural affair, but any unsettling of the priestly power base reached beyond the religious realm. The Jewish and Roman authorities functioned in a symmetry carefully maintained by particular arrangements. When Jesus cleansed the temple of money changers, it was a multidimensional event. The priests held political appointment and thus a challenge to their integrity affected a network beyond the religious sphere. An assault on religious practice vibrates into the corridors of the city hall. It is significant that "those who dominated the religion of Israel, and hence the social configuration of the nation's life, saw Jesus as a dangerous enemy threatening their public preeminence."¹⁰ The final confirmation of the threat is in the manner of his death. Crucifixion was the fate of political criminals and subversives; stoning was for blasphemy. To those who held power, religious and political, Jesus represented a challenge to their authority. The powers responded with the manner of death appropriate to the crime.

Sometimes the challenge to social formation is more subtle. The interplay between Jesus, Mary, and Martha is illustrative. An examination of the social context reveals a liberation component. Martha invited Jesus into her home. Her sister, Mary, "sat at the Lord's feet and listened to his teachings" while Martha was in the kitchen performing the household chores. When she challenged the actions of Mary, Jesus replied, "Mary has chosen the good portion" (Luke 10:38–42). On the surface one would think Martha's call for fair play was met with Jesus' affirmation of Mary's good judgment, but the force of his response is missed in that analysis. Mary was violating a structure of the society. It was not appropriate for a woman to be in a learning relationship to a rabbi. Her role was in the kitchen. In commending Mary, Jesus sided with her challenge. His response "broke open and transformed the social structures of the world in which he lived." He refused to honor the structures of society that blocked her "journey toward freedom."

It is futile to pursue the New Testament records in search of a model of Jesus either as a political activist or as mired in aspirations for change in persons. One can speculate that "had social conditions been transformable in the first century in a way similar to what is now possible through appropriate technological and socioeconomic policies, Jesus would most likely have demanded such a transformation and acted to bring it about."[11] But this is to manipulate history and violate its particularity. The issue is: What agenda is set in our time by Jesus' message and ministry?

It is enough for us to know that in the biblical setting the priority is with the actualization of freedom, which has both personal and structual components. Whether the new person or the new society comes first in the New Testament is an "ahistorical" question.

D. One Story or Another

The argument drawn from biblical precedents is that we cannot choose between social and personal transformation. Both self and structure "constitute an inseparable unity."[12] Liberation in one sphere without corresponding change in another is neither lasting nor durable. We are formed and deformed from within and from without. But the issue remains, which comes first? The problem with that question is that there are no grounds for resolving it—in the abstract, a case can be made as persuasively for the one as for the other.

Choosing between the new person and the new society may not be necessary, but a beginning is. In any particular time and place we approach the Christian tradition with one story or another. The circumstances of the age enable, and finally require, a choice. There is a context within which interpretation takes place. "No man has direct access to the contents of Scripture either by the perfection of his scholarship or the power of his inspiration."[13] We come to it with full hands; what we bear with us determines what we receive.

Paul Tillich made a distinction between the sources and the norm in the development of a theology. Obviously, the sources are those to which one turns. For Tillich they were the Bible, church history, the history of religion and culture. The norm determines the use of the sources. The norm is "the criterion to which the sources . . . must be subjected."[14] By its very nature the norm in any era emerges through an essentially unconscious process; it appears rather than is produced. The norm guides interpretation of the sources. Tillich expressed his norm in these terms: "It is not an exaggeration to say that today man experiences his present situation in terms of disruption, conflict, self-destruction, meaninglessness, and despair in all realms of life."[15] The human story for Tillich, at least at the time of that writing, was formed in terms of the self and the need for a new being. It can be argued, parenthetically, that when Tillich was in Germany he formulated the issue in more social terms.

The version of the human story with which one enters the sources affects the message one hears from them. With self-estrangement the issue, the "New Being" and the "New Creation" become the dominant themes. However, "Reading the Bible with the eyes of the poor is a different thing from reading it with the eyes of the man with a full belly . . . in the light of the experience of the hopes of the oppressed, the Bible's revolutionary themes—promise, exodus, resurrection and the Spirit—come alive."[16]

Liberation theology is, of course, concerned with the self and its traumas. Any forfeiture and compromise with the individual finally defeats the intentions of the biblical message. But a true understanding of the individual is always

"inconceivable apart from a social context."[17] In our time
the force of our experience calls for a story that embraces
the full range of social patterns. The actualization of freedom is bound up more directly with our social systems and
institutions than with the existential anguish within us. We
seem to be more at the mercy of events in the social order
than of the inner sanctum. Some of the words that evoke
the strongest emotional responses are not echoes from our
interiors—though they reverberate there. The code words
for our most vexing distresses are not guilt, meaninglessness, or death, but Watergate, Iran, Vietnam, boat people,
assassination, OPEC, CIA, FBI, starvation, sexism, racism, Attica, Middle East, police brutality, inflation, crime.

These words raise in systemic terms the issues of a new
history and the openness of the future. The actualization of
freedom forms around the use of power in our society. The
negations of humanity and the affirmations of the humane
are both bound up with the power of institutions and systems over our lives. For us now the pursuit and practice of
freedom in history are political. What is being done to us in
the social order limits our freedom more than do internal
restraints. In the face of that, personal initiatives, while
important, seem pitifully inadequate. Perhaps we can adapt
the norm set down by Tillich: "It is not an exaggeration to
say that today men experience their present situation in
terms of corruption, oppression, destructive agencies, systemic futility, and political manipulations in all realms of
life." That is the public story in terms of which our private
story is lived and conceived. Only a version of the Christian
faith written with our structural conditions in view will
address and be adequate to our contemporary experience.
A Gospel addressed to changed social conditions is a predicate for changed lives.

Chapter 1 explores two stories of liberation—the story of
Sara and Abraham and the story of the transfiguration.
Each is an authentic and forceful narrative of the actualization of freedom. One describes freedom in terms of personal transformation; the other portrays freedom at issue in
the contest between a new order about to be born and an

old one not yet ready to die. Hope is a factor in each story, as are a new history and openness to the future. For liberation theology there is no need to choose between the narratives but, beginning from below, in our experience of our time and place, there is a need to rank them. It is in the context of the transfiguration that we can fully understand ourselves as Sara and Abraham. Our journey toward freedom occurs as the social forces surrounding us are turned from oppression, humiliation, and deprivation. The hungry will be fed, the unemployed enabled to work, the political prisoners released, the demeaned will find their possibilities, and the victims of discrimination their value when the biblical message is expressed in the context of our experiences in the social order. Then the passage from Christ to a troubled world will be possible.

Notes

1. Peter Berger, *The Sacred Canopy* (Garden City, N.Y.: Doubleday, 1967), pp. 3–4.
2. Ibid., pp. 4–25.
3. Ibid., p. 4.
4. Ibid., p. 11.
5. Ibid., p. 9.
6. Ibid., p. 11.
7. Ibid., p. 17.
8. Dorthee Söelle, *Political Theology* (Philadelphia: Fortress Press, 1974), p. 65.
9. Ignacio Ellacuria, *Freedom Made Flesh* (Maryknoll, N.Y.: Orbis Books, 1976), p. 30.
10. Ibid., pp. 31–32.
11. Peter C. Hodgson, *New Birth of Freedom* (Philadelphia: Fortress Press, 1976), p. 242.
12. Ibid., p. 308.
13. James D. Smart, *The Strange Silence of the Bible in the Church* (Philadelphia: Westminster Press, 1970), p. 53.
14. Paul Tillich, *Systematic Theology*, vol. 1 (University of Chicago Press, 1951), p. 47.
15. Ibid., p. 49.
16. Jürgen Moltmann, *The Church in the Power of the Spirit* (New York: Harper and Row, 1977), p. 17.
17. Söelle, *Political Theology*, p. 43.

6 Stories and the Future

Stories of economic self-interest and the sufficiency of the individual conspire to design the future for the benefit of the few while presuming to render it open for the many. Frontier and Horatio Alger stories shape our consciousness and lead to the conviction that there is no need to change the system when it is individuals who are found wanting. These stories are sustained and gain momentum when joined to the story behind American civil religion. It sacralizes the goodness of the established order, the confidence that social mobility exists, and the "benevolent" distribution of power. When story is gathered up in story, the effect is maintenance of the status quo. We are led to accept the world as it is, to be concerned with gradually righting its wrongs, and to envision a world that grows out of present conditions.

These stories all convey an ideology widely accepted in our society. An ideology is a system of ideas that functions to interpret for us the way life is. Ideologies are part of our value systems that govern, often unconsciously, the formation of our sense of self and its relation to the whole of the social fabric. Ideologies are "disclosure models of reality" that provide "compelling reinterpretations of the meaning of events and the drift of the human project."[1] They enable us to get our bearings in the social context.

The story and ideology into which most of us have been socialized develops something like this: we live in a society that has been carefully conceived by our forefathers. Its systems and institutions exist for high purposes, such as the preservation of individual freedom. From time to time the

150

need arises for them to be adapted to a different era. That process is best achieved in an evolutionary manner. Severe disruption violates the dynamic of community, which has as its goals the provision of harmonizing relationships. Those individuals within society who sense the need for change should not raise their voices in strident echoes of dissent. It is important that we learn to "reason together" and leave passion and rage for the animals. Reasonable people can dispassionately view the limits in all social systems but recognize as well that they only exist for our own welfare. Nothing is accomplished and the society is not well served when we violate law and order. In our society there are innumerable systems and institutions that serve the common good. We must be careful, however, to keep each in its appropriate place. The church, for example, is intended for the spiritual realm; it ought not make moves into the political sphere. It should console the individual. A good person can and should exert influence within the system. Personal virtue is what matters. Good persons make for good government. Our attention should focus on affirming the American traditions and rituals that nourish the individual into high values and an appropriate place in society. There are, of course, many times when we must yield to the common good and sacrifice our preferences. We gladly receive the benefits of life in our society; we must boldly accept the responsibilities. Citizens have to pay their dues.

That is the conventional wisdom shared through the ages. The story affirms that our institutions are benign and benevolent, the wise among us reason rather than rage, harmony is the clue to whatever change might be needed, and confidence and patience with processes are the signs of maturity.

In our contemporary society there are several code words that express this story with particular intensity for the individual consciousness. Certainly one is the priority given to *security*. The phenomenon of "securitism" is described by Martin Marty as "the adjusted set of expectations which leads people to set forth only modest goals for changes, based on the issue of how little change will unsettle existing institutions."[2] It is easy to understand a recoil from the disposition to risk and dream. Defense against change follows calls for change. Many feel they have been pressured long enough to act against their will. They become weary of "movements" with their manipulative dynamics, deaf to strident tones in discourse, and immune to the polarizing issues of the day. The desire for stability at any price—to someone else—serves well the desire for security.

Another code word is *realism*. Realism is facing up to things as they "really are." The summons to "be realistic" is an invitation to withdraw from a dream world and cope with existence as given. The claim is that such realism represents a summons or a path to freedom. A person whose head is directed by another world is a victim of fantasies. Personal and social self-limitation is the only way to live in touch with reality. One ought not waste one's energies on what won't work, what will never be. The wise person accepts the facts at hand and arranges them in the best way possible. It is important to operate in relation to the rules of the game and not become fanciful with one's expectations. Politics is the art of the possible and the individual of merit and consequence is one who makes the best of what is given. To play with the possible, not the impossible, is the measure of maturity and responsibility. It is also the form of our complicity in preventing a new future for others.

Oddly enough, another code word is *cynicism*. It would seem to contradict the importance of realism in the scenario above, but it is a twisted version of the sense of permanence of systems and institutions that underlies the cry to be realistic. The brand of cynicism at large fixes on institutions that are bent and will never be any other way, on individuals' unwillingness and inability to transcend self-interest, on the assumption that basically no good can come of humankind and society. Securitism and realism play into cynicism. The adjusted set of expectations supposedly based upon the way things really are leads us to function free from anticipation that our common life could ever be other than it is. We are convinced that very little can be done and that we deceive ourselves if we spend our energies in assessments and dreams that tell a different story. When one analyzes the conventional wisdom into which we are socialized, one finds that what is fundamental to our experience is futurelessness. Everythings ends with the message that what is, will be. "Wild, irrational hope" is extinguished at every point in our experience. Obviously, futurelessness has its more poignant forms in the continued existence and virulence of racism, sexism, and Third World realities, but they do not exhaust the phenomenon. We are all taught to envision what lies at hand as the only utopia we can expect. The story we are told begins and ends in place.

A. Immersion in the Present

One of the forces in modern industrial society that binds us most decisively to present arrangements is bureaucratization. Large bureaucratic organizations are concerned with their survival, which can be assured under conditions of economic growth in an otherwise stable environment. For industrial societies, preservation of the status quo is not just an expression of an overweening conservatism or an irrational resistance to change. Rather, it is a response to the basic notion that instability disturbs that distribution of power, wealth, and income that ensures the continued status of an organizational elite. It is in the interests of the few to have the way things are set the agenda for how things will be. Any sense of a future that breaks in and breaks up the present must be avoided through whatever forms of immersion in the present are available.

Robert Heilbroner has pointed out that all industrial societies, whether nominally capitalist or socialist, are characterized by bureaucratic organization. Therefore, they find it difficult to respond to crises that call for fundamental changes in the structure of society.[3] The complex economic activity of an advanced industrialized nation is such that the decision-making apparatus must become bureaucratic. The large-scale risk taking required to build a modern steel industry, for example, must be spread out and protected by a system of group expertise in the decision-making process. This point has led Galbraith to develop the notion of the "planning system."[4] That system must be a part of a successful large-scale industrialization process. The industrialization may occur largely in and through the private sector and create a "corporate" bureaucracy or it may occur in the public sector and create a "state" bureaucracy. Indeed, in either case there will almost certainly develop a parallel political bureaucracy that will set the proper climate of stability for the success of the productive bureaucracy.

As group decision making replaces that of the individual, it is only natural that protection of a group's existence and status becomes a crucial element in its decision-making process. Individual risk takers may be willing to make radical changes because the individual rewards for such actions can be great. Such thinking must, in part, have motivated the actions of the nineteenth-century industrial and colonial empire builders as well as the leaders of the Russian Revolution. Bold individual actions were effective in bringing about drastic changes in the economic, political, and social fabrics of their societies. For the bureaucratic, modern, industrial society, the group that is responsible for a given set of decisions has already attained a significant degree of status and power; its decision making must always take into account the maintenance of position. A strong orientation toward stability is a consistent thread running through all of the actions and decisions made by such bureaucracies.

The drive for stability maintains the existing power balance among groups in the society. Those who have been systematically excluded from a share of the power, income, wealth, and status find themselves with no effective systemic remedies for redressing their situations. Two further difficulties loom in the face of these structures. First, the immersion in the present of the bureaucracies makes it very difficult for them to envision a future system significantly different from the present one. As a result, even "good-hearted" bureaucrats find themselves powerless to effect any real changes that will create a different and more promising future for the excluded groups and persons. We have had "equal pay for equal work" laws on the books for at least fifteen years at the federal level, yet there has been very little real change in the working conditions and/or income status of women in the labor force. The law only addresses one of the symptoms of job discrimination. The overwhelming majority in the bureaucratic structure finds an increased role for women in the system as a threat to its power and status and reacts accordingly. This is not primarily a sexist response. The bureaucracies will react this way with regard to any "out" group because disturbing the existing distribution of power and status is not desirable.

The second problem inherent in the bureaucracy is an inability to anticipate future crises. The system seems to respond reasonably well to any current crisis, provided that responses do not require any wrenching change in structure. The cold war and the space race are precisely the kinds of problems that bring out the best in the productive bureaucracy. A chance to apply and extend various technologies to new problems is at the heart of the acknowledged success of industrial society. Where the real impact of a problem will clearly be felt in the future, and its magnitude calls for reorientation of values and restructuring of economic relationships, industrial socieites do not respond effectively.

All of the industrial nations of the world have felt the impact of the energy crisis. This crisis is, in its current structure, largely manufactured by OPEC actions that artificially restrict supply and raise the price of oil. Since the technologies of industrial nations are oil-energy dependent, such a restriction has triggered worldwide economic problems including extensive unemployment and pervasive inflation. This would seem like a problem tailor-made for the bureaucratic system with its ability to apply technology to problems and find new solutions. The difficulty is that the "crisis" is a future crisis, not a present one. There is still sufficient oil to provide for all of the needs of those who are willing and able to pay. Ability to pay has never been a problem for the productive bureaucracies whose monopolistic structures enable them to pass on the cost in the form of higher prices. As long as "business as usual" can be maintained without changing structures or technologies, the system, immersed in the present, will not effect significant change. Industrial societies may be incapable of preparing now for the time when the supply of fossil fuels is restricted to a point that calls for wrenching changes in energy consumption and productive techniques.

In a similar vein, a series of court decisions and legislative actions have firmly established the principle that segregation in education works to the detriment of black students and extends the conditions that have led to reduced economic, political, and social status. A straightforward application of distribution theory would reduce the clustering of blacks in certain schools and would thus eliminate the de facto segregation that is the focus of the current concern. The impact of the desegregation will be felt in the future as increased productivity for black citizens results from an overall improvement in educational quality. Once again, using the tools and techniques of the productive bureaucracy has not achieved the desired changes in the system. There are probably two reasons for this. The payoff—increased productivity—is a societal benefit and, contrary to the neoclassical story, individuals do not gain enough personally to make the requisite sacrifices. Also, it is difficult to plan for an alternate future in which the current distributions of power, wealth, and status are disturbed. That does not necessarily imply selfishness, but a vision of the current system as the right one and any profound disturbance as clearly wrong. The impact of these attitudes is that educational desegregation is accomplished only with conspicuous reluctance, usually with acrimony, and often with violence. Rather than having school districts use their abilities and economic resources to achieve high-quality integrated education by means of imaginative and exciting use of all of the tools and techniques of modern society, we find ourselves in the United States battling every effort to bring about such changes. A significant part of this unrelenting refusal to extend quality education to all must stem from the fear of a future that may be different from the present most find so comfortable.

There is a similarity between the energy crisis and the desegregation problem. In energy the real physical shortages will come in the future, and in desegregation the productivity payoff and the changed economic status will lie in the future as well. The various bureaucracies have had enormous difficulty developing a workable policy for accomplishing changes that will allow us to accommodate these expected or desired future conditions. They represent such drastic changes in existing systemic structures that the bureaucracies find it extremely difficult to do what is necessary.

That is a particularly interesting conclusion to draw about the capitalist bureaucracies since investment and effective planning for the future are the lifeblood of success. Unfortunately, the future for which these bureaucracies plan is an extension of the present they dominate. When the vision of the future is no longer a linear extension of the present, their planning mechanism breaks down. For example, so much of our industrial structure is built upon oil that it is a very wrenching experience for the productive bureaucracy even to contemplate a future in which the availability of oil is so restricted that wholly new production techniques have to be devised. A bureaucracy immersed in the present system and in present techniques will be unable to plan effectively for a different future. When the future can only be an extension of the present structure, the range of possibilities is closed down and the system fails to accommodate to change. This can lead to a collapse of the institutional structures as the pressure of radically altered conditions comes to bear upon an inadequately prepared bureaucratic system.

In the United States, the neoclassical story plays an important role in providing some of the stability necessary for survival of the system. It is in the best interests of the bureaucratic structures to have private ownership and accumulation, which allow them to effectively control the use of productive resources to serve the needs of the bureaucracy. The competitive neoclassical analysis tells a story of the economic system in which self-interested acts serve social needs; widespread belief in the story protects the bureaucracy at its most vulnerable point.

The potential for providing for the material needs of human beings is great within industrial societies. Immersion in the present and belief in outmoded stories dulls and often eliminates the capacity of such societies to distribute the fruits of their production in any new way that might better serve that human need. And it is precisely in the area where such systems do their job best—production decision making—that they invariably sanction the present most completely.

The problem of urban transportation in the United States provides an example. We clearly have an overreliance on private automobiles, which leads to a waste of both energy and time and contributes significantly to urban air pollution. There must be practical alternatives to the single-rider vehicle with the internal combustion engine that can provide efficient urban transport. Who is going to decide which is the best alternative? Suppose the Ford Motor Company decides that the proper alternative is electric buses and it conducts research and invests in the development of fast, efficient, and reliable buses. However, having a better idea is not enough; Ford will be rewarded only if it can convince *everyone* it is right. Faced with high development costs and uncertain rewards, the planning bureaucracies of most large corporations will opt for maintenance of the status quo; the internal combustion engine will remain dominant. If the political bureaucracy attempts to solve the problem by establishing a national transportation policy, the vested interests in the private sector will resist this infringement on their rights. They will perceive it as an attempt to upset the existing balance of power and status. Indeed, it will be difficult for the political bureaucracy even to establish a worthwhile policy, let alone enforce it. The legislative and executive interplay required to achieve national policy almost naturally calls for the intervention of the private corporate and labor bureaucracies, each seeking to maintain its position in the face of potential change.[5] This creates a powerful sense of inertia that seriously limits the possibilities for meaningful alternatives. As a result, we have no national transportation, energy, environmental, income-distribution, or educational policies. This is not due to a lack of widespread concern about these issues, but rather to a continuing inertia caused by the interplay among the vested interest groups and the bureaucracies to which they give rise.

Such problems are by no means endemic to capitalist systems; the socialist and centrally planned economies also fail to solve them effectively. But it appears that they may be more difficult to solve in capitalist systems, if only because significant change requires the confluence of so many private interests. From another perspective, the ability of our system to deal with any problem is immense. The most recent outstanding example is the successes of our space programs. Why is it that that same expertise and organizational talent cannot be used to solve problems of poverty, discrimination, and environmental protection?[6] In part it is the specter of changed structures attached to such problems that inhibits creative and imaginative solutions. In addition, the neoclassical story with its belief in the efficacy of the market further weakens the ability of the system to respond.

The essential feature of the neoclassical economic model is that the market meets the need for change. If transportation alternatives are really needed, this will be signaled by a decreased demand for and use of private automobiles and an increased use of public transportation. This alerts the entrepreneurs in the system that research and investment in alternative means of transportation may yield a profitable return. Alternatively, the high prices and current shortages of conventional energy resources will lead entrepreneurs to use their management expertise to work out alternative energy sources.

The market does not always achieve this redirection of effort. The widespread existence of monopoly power distorts both market signals and the response to those signals. As a result, large corporations and labor unions that produce transportation equipment, build highways, and sell gasoline may band together to protect their vested interests and subvert alternative transportation systems. The belief that the market will find the best and most efficient solutions seriously weakens any nonmarket efforts to achieve change in the system. Once again, belief in the story blinds us to the fact that there are many situations where the pure market system does not work at all, or only works inefficiently.

Part of the failure to respond well to certain crises rests with our confidence in the market as a vehicle for change. Market solutions to problems do reflect consumer choices to some degree, and to this extent failure to respond to crisis reflects widespread failure to recognize it. However, the market also responds strongly to the existing distribution of income and economic power. Market solutions echo the interests of those who already have the lion's share of income, wealth, and economic power in the society. The self-interests of these groups help to dictate the solutions that the market will find to given problems and situations. The unequal distribution of income and wealth and the existence of monopoly power thwart the efforts of Adam Smith's "invisible hand" to achieve maximum social welfare from the pursuit of individual self-interest. It is natural that the self-interested responses of power groups to crisis will be an attempt to "hold the line" in order to maintain their power. The difficulty in getting rational, change-oriented responses to crisis is further compounded by the fact that this oligopoly of economic power rests not in the hands of individuals but in the hands of impersonal corporate decision-making organizations, large labor unions, and political bureaucracies.

If bureaucracies enable the present to preside over the future, how might an alternate future begin to be shaped in the present? What is the substance to the claim signaled in the transfiguration story that there is a countdown on whose world this is and whose will is to prevail?

B. The Vocation for Freedom

Liberation theology is capable of envisioning real change and the prospects of that change occurring. Its methodology requires that we take the measure of our experience in history. Theology from below leads us to define our world from within our experience. There can be no prior knowledge of where we are such as that given to us by our ideologies, stories, and institutions. What we have always known may, of course, be a significant resource for expressing where we are. What we experience in society precedes what we know in doctrine, and is our point of entry into the content of faith. As is argued in chapter 1, liberation theology has been formed around the categories of oppressed and oppressors. Sexist, racist, and Third World categories have given both form and content to that theology. But the majority of us are not oppressed, and it is difficult to see where we go with the identity of oppressors. Can there be more to our existence than waiting to be overthrown, or perhaps encouraging it? Biblical notions of waiting are more active and creative than that. Perhaps it is possible to reach around those categories—without renouncing them—and identify a component within our personal experience.

A line attributed to Gabriel Marcel calls back into focus

what can happen to the individual: "The child in me dies a little day-by-day. Had I been a poet it would not have been so." While Marcel's reference may be to the process of aging, the experience need not be limited to that. For most of us, the life process in society is a progressive contraction of the imagination. The facility for envisioning other terms than those existent dries up, leaving a personal desert. The death of the child in us is the demise of aspiration for an alternate future—it no longer seems possible. The tyranny of the particular has not suffocated the child's imagination; children play with all the possibilities. A child would rejoice in the news of Sara and Abraham's prospect for an offspring; "wild, irrational hope" needs no proof or rationale. But, alas, "the child in me dies" and we live by prediction not by promise. The "cold logic of human reason" is in force, foreclosing on any future beyond an extension of the present. The story of futurelessness presides over the imagination.

The rekindling of "wild, irrational hope" may begin with individuals. Persons can be subjects who control the formation of their history. To be a subject means to take responsibility for one's destiny and to rebel against domination. The subject status of many in our society has been eroded by submission in our institutional setting. Acceptance of the comfort that comes from knowing and having a "place" leads one to restrain imagination and become an object. Our ontological vocation "to be a subject who acts upon and transforms his world, and in so doing moves toward ever new possibilities of a fuller and richer life individually and collectively"[7] is forfeited and taken from us.

While a "fear of freedom" may restrain, Paulo Freire argues that human beings can be restored to their ontological vocation. Those in whom futurelessness has taken hold can undergo a painful process of rebirth. They can "perceive the reality of oppression not as a closed world from which there is no exit, but as a limiting situation which they can transform."[8] The process of rebirth begins with "unveiling" their condition as futurelessness. Action will come from critical reflection and the embracing of responsibility. To be born again means to think differently about ourselves and refuse the submersion of our selfhood in the situation. Decisions once again become personal and are no longer controlled by ideology and institutions. Intervention and a new future become possibilities, and submission the sign of inauthentic existence. When the story of futurelessness is told against our experience of it, it can set in motion the process of emerging as a subject. Within that contention is an assumption about our nature: we are creatures who name what is absent and rebel against what is present.

To say that we name what is absent means that we can live from a horizon rather than within the immediacy of experience. We are not content with what lies at hand. We imagine and anticipate what does not exist. Reality is not defined solely by the form and substance of the present. We are animated by what is missing, and in response to the staleness of the moment we envision something new. In the words of Theodore Roszak, humankind proclaims "a new heaven and earth so vast, so marvelous that the inordinate claims of technical expertise must of necessity withdraw in the presence of such splendor to a subordinate and marginal status in the lives of men. . . . There are eyes which see it transformed, made lustrous beyond measure."[9] Refusing to submit to the verdict of the present, human beings are impassioned by what is absent. The existing state of things is not the outer limit of imagination. We dream things that never were rather than be devoured by what is. We resist accommodation to the way things are. Our logic is of the heart and the imagination.

The other side of human nature is that it resists what is present. Aspiration for a new future is generated by futurelessness. We react to the negation of humanity by wanting to negate the negative. Because we can name what is absent, we rebel against what is present. In a sense, hope is generated by hopelessness; knowing that things are not as they could be, we lash out at the restraints.

In the biblical record, those in captivity have the soul for vision. Suffering in, above, and finally against the present, they become agents of a new future. It is not incidental that Isaiah plays upon the theme of a suffering servant and the New Testament writers grasp that image to represent the event of Christ. The liberator is not a king on a throne but a servant on a cross.

The prospects of resistance are born in suffering the present. The oppressed can know that current structures are not the last word; reality is other than the illusions of the "real world"; what is possible in any moment of time goes beyond a refinement of what is actual. Suffering from futurelessness, they may begin responding to those who deny their humanity. The search for a home begins in homelessness. Naming the absence of peace causes us to act out our protest against the presence of war; naming the absence of equality causes us to respond to the forces of racism; naming the demise of civil liberties causes us to conspire against the system.

To interpret humankind in terms of the future is to understand ourselves as a "creature who hopes." We name what is missing; we rebel against what is present. But is that enough for confidence that a new future is attainable? Not really; our hope collapses against itself. Durable change is an ongoing process rather than a climactic moment. The same person who strives for what is missing and rebels against the futurelessness and hopelessness of the present can renege on the future. One can cease to hold oneself to the attainment of the qualitatively new. The horizon that has informed our understanding is drawn in and in time coincides with the present. We copy the past rather than create a future. We no longer dream dreams but romanticize the commonplace. As for the rebellion, that can be easily bought off. A few strategic concessions can and have restored the rebel to the position of a happy slave. We can be domesticated and neutralized without ever having the shackles of futurelessness seriously impaired. There is nothing about our nature that holds us to the future. We cannot sustain ourselves as poets.

The story of revolt against futurelessness can be authentic, but it is incomplete. Another story can be added to this one, completing and sustaining it.

C. The Resurrection Story

The stories we are told engender futurelessness. The story we might tell ourselves is an invitation to stand out and redefine our future. The biblical story of the Resurrection centers on a future already broken open for us. It moves beyond our "ontological vocation" to a claim about our history. That makes possible agenda setting that is free from the shackles of the existing order.

The list of preachers sent to jail for their Easter sermons is not long, but the precedent is early and distinguished. "And as Peter and John were speaking to the people, the priests and the captain of the Temple and the Sadducees came upon them, annoyed because they were . . . proclaiming in Jesus the resurrection from the dead. And they arrested them" (Acts 4:1–3). Proclaiming the Resurrection and civil arrests do not appear to have a natural connection. Perhaps Peter and John were really about something else and the line was drawn tight when they happened to be preaching. But the word *annoyed* hangs between the two events. In English it is soft; *annoyed* may equal a minor irritant. The Greek word implies a deeper vexation. While its usages are few, other contexts suggest both pain caused to the body and mental grief.[10] The depth of meaning in the word is focused by those who were involved. The priests and the captain had earthbound capacity for control. Their stake was in the present, with all the futurelessness it may represent. The priests, far from being monkish holy men, held civil positions and were the aristocracy in their society. Within Judaism the Sadducees, closely tied to the rich and influential, were bound to the Pentateuch as the source of their authority and thus preserved "authentic" tradition against the ravages of liberals. The captain of the Temple, not just a director of security, had at his command an armed guard with law and order as their sacred mission. That which "annoyed" them cut across their authority and power over the present arrangements. Their systems of control were being threatened by another vision of history. Their ability to foreclose upon the future was canceled in the proclamation of the Resurrection.

The classic move with any brand or dimension of eschatology (doctrines of the end) is toward one's personal survival. The existential point of entry accents personal decision about our destiny as offered in Christ. Recent moves in theology brought eschatology into the present as a moment of personal opportunity. "The *eschaton* did not lie in the future of history but in the present of each human subject."[11] That is threat enough, both to those who fear human decision making and those who recoil from that process within themselves. But the meaning is larger than that. The priests, Sadducees, and captains of the temple knew it instinctively. Enemies of the Gospel often catch its drift more decisively than friends. The Resurrection means that history can get out of hand and that the "cold logic of human reason" forged to systems and institutions need not prevail. The future can hold its own in the present. Principalities and powers work against that.

The word *future* functions in two different and contradictory ways. For some it is an effect; for others it is a cause. For some it is what may be reasonably expected, given what is known; for others, it is what may be reasonably anticipated, given what is believed. For some it is a Barbie doll traded in on a new and improved Barbie doll; for others it is a virgin giving birth. For some it is a result of intelligent planning, and for others it is a rebirth of wonder and imagination.

The first and more common function of the word is to specify what will be on the basis of present tendencies. As in Alvin Toffler's usage, the future is a projection from the conditions and prospects at hand. It is something we know "for the most part"—a refinement and extension of the present. We know about what to expect because we are now in the midst of the forces that determine it. But in Ernst Bloch's writings, for example, the word functions differently. The future is itself a cause; it has what he calls "ontological priority." The present hinges on it. The sequence of events is reversed. What will be molds and informs what is. The future is not something we "know for the most part" but something we only "know in part." It is the stage of the qualitatively new, the unexpectable, where the surprises occur. The future is not an extension of the present, but doubles back on it, giving the present its reality, its dynamism, and its immediate possibilities. Israel did not know what the coming of the Messiah would be like; but the coming Messiah taught Israel what the present could be like. The future led the present out of bondage. Biblically, the future is something by which we are conditioned, not something into which we are conditioned.

When Peter and John proclaimed the resurrection in Christ, they were heard as announcing that the future would not be of the making of the priests, Sadducees, and captains of the temple. The future was not only open but its openness impacted the present formations of power and authority.

The Resurrection story backs up our "ontological vocation" with a claim about our history. Our story fits into a story where "breaking in and breaking up" are the consequence of more action than our own. On Good Friday it was all over, or so it seemed to the disciples. They fled. Imagine their despair and disillusionment as the boundary of death took shape on a cross. They could not realistically expect any of the things they had come to believe were possible. But the "God of hope" (Romans 15:13) did not leave it there with all the possibilities played out. On Easter morning the foreclosed future was liberated. The futurelessness that bound the consciousness of the disciples was shattered, making anticipation and imagination possible again. Under these conditions persons again have opened to them the possibility of being subjects; naming

their own history in an open field becomes an option. The
dying child in one's center comes to life again. Dreams for
the world and the confidence to enact them emerge. The
future takes over in the orchestration of the present. The
promises of God enable persons to begin living against the
very things that have lived against them. In the enactment
of one's life, one can become a poet.

D. The Storytelling Community

Stories are finally believable only in the midst of a community in which they are believed. Personal contact is, of
course, always essential; without it, stories are only in circulation. Each of us has significant jurisdiction over
whether or not they are invoked and ingested as our own
story. The individual cannot be preempted as the reference
point. Persons make decisions unless their submersion is so
complete that any intervention in their history is precluded.
Being a subject is being able to say "I"; the "Single One"
whom Kierkegaard and Buber said has a self-solidarity out
of which one can name, declare, and commit oneself. "No
one is excluded from being a Single One except him who
excludes himself by wishing to be 'crowd'."[12] Yet "concrete singularity" occurs in relationships. Singularity
emerges in the presence of others, paradoxically, not without them. "The courage to be as oneself" and "the courage
to be as a part" are intertwined; "self-affirmation necessarily includes the affirmation of oneself as a participant."[13]
There is no singularity without solidarity; in the profoun-
dest sense we can only be a child in the midst of children
and our stories only make sense to us in the measure that
their sense is embraced by a community.

As has been argued, stories contain "models of reality."
Anything related even tangentially to reality or truth or
knowledge has at the very least a social construction. There
is a "relationship between human thought and the social
context within which it arises" that we overlook only in

self-delusion.[14] Our awarenesses in any form are acquired and supported through a socializing process. Plausibility is related to social legitimation. The point is that when individuals make decisions about stories, the believability of the stories is contextual. One can only believe them in the presence of others who find them believable. That is true of every story. The stories we tell ourselves by ourselves cannot finally hold and shape our lives.

Part of the human problem, then, is always where we place ourselves. One can accept one's place in the center of the prevailing drama of futurelessness and even can believe it furthers our possibilities as persons, but nothing in that story enables the emergence of the child within us. Or we can be among those who affirm our "ontological vocation" to be subjects through awareness of oppression. But the ability to "stand out" in the strength of our vocation is suspect. The alternative is to be where the Resurrection story, with its affirmation that the future is forever broken open for us, is told. Then our aspiration to be subject is caught up in the processes of intervention beyond ourselves. The Resurrection story is attractive; who wouldn't want "reality" to be cooperative in our journey toward freedom? Making the story our own is the burden we bear, and that raises the issue of the church.

Dismay over the quality of the church's existence in our experience can obscure its essential and incorruptible mission. One cannot deny that the wrong stories can be told within the church. Memorial Day celebrations in the sanctuary and at the cemetery convey more often than not the story of American civil religion—usually the society's pride in striving, competition, and success are echoed with astonishing frequency. Distortion and displacement of the biblical message are persistent and pervasive. The message gets lost as other stories are amplified and sacralized. All of that and more occurs within the temple, but the church is as well the place where the right stories are available.

What distinguishes the church, and is the basis of hope in the human project, is its existence as the place where the story of Christ is narrated. It has at hand a story of liberation even when its common life and existence in the public sphere negates it. The authority of the story is secure even when misunderstood and muted by the culture-bound stories at large. Something *can* happen when the right story is told. The church may have the capacity to create the experience that it addresses. Jürgen Moltmann refers to the church as the " 'story-telling fellowship', which continually wins its own freedom from the stories and myths of the society in which it lives, from the present realization of this story of Christ."[15] The church, even in its most fragile form, is the place where the language exists through which the Gospel of freedom can be heard. When social activist Saul Alinsky was asked why his work was so frequently initiated and sustained by the churches and synagogues, he replied that the communities of the Judeo-Christian faith had the stories of freedom that were magnets to claims for change. The right stories were there to challenge the economic structures that limited vision and closed down a new future.

The church as "storytelling fellowship" on the surface might seem at odds with the arguments of a social construction of reality. It has to be conceded that fidelity to the biblical story may be faint and allegiance to others more secure. There is an assumption that the story of Christ has an authority of its own—less than that would preclude the input of the Holy Spirit—but the argument moves beyond, claiming the story has authority within the church even when its use and message are impaired. The people of the church have an attachment to the story even when its meaning eludes them. "The church is not what it seems to be in any one time or place. It is always the bearer of the sources of its own transformation. It even carries under the surface explosive materials."[16] The Resurrection story is told within the church and believed to be essential to the faith within the church. It is the only place to hear and recognize the status of the future. The church is where the corrections take place, where in the power of the Resurrection story a people win freedom from stories of inauthentic existence.

It is in the church that the child in us can be born again. Even when its own story is of a withering imagination, its telling of the Resurrection story keeps alive the authority of the future over the present. There we can say together "by His great mercy we have been born anew to a living hope through the Resurrection of Jesus Christ" (I Peter 1:3). And in the telling of that story with one another its legitimacy may take hold, enabling us to be transformed from the future and under its impact rearrange the present.

In the biblical tradition the promises of God take hold within the people of God. For faith there is no first person. We may say "I believe," but it is a universal *I*. The creeds are statements of a community of faith. My *I* stands with all the *I*'s in the history of Israel and the church and only has its force in that social context. The "God of hope" is embraced by a people who together "abound in hope." Christians take their place in church because that is where the promises of God in the Resurrection are available and may be taken seriously. Consequently, that is where the prospect exists of overcoming futurelessness. Under the impact of the Resurrection story, the church is the body of people who refuse to put up with things as they are presently arranged. As a consequence of telling the story, Christians believe the lovelessness in life can and will be overcome by decency and dignity in our history; the injustices that deprive persons of a viable existence can and will be overcome by a quality of justice that affirms the rightful claims persons have in our world; the cycles of hate and animosity that so viciously destroy can and will be overcome by a graciousness enabling reunion with those we have offended; the sicknesses of mind and body that drain the vestiges of hope from us can and will be overcome by healing powers that make us whole again. Promises become real and their fulfillment becomes our responsibility when, within the "storytelling fellowship," we retell the story as our own. Then the message of the Resurrection will have worked in us a journey toward freedom we could not ourselves have begun or sustained. The dominance of their story assures the constant critical stance that is essential to prevent the reemergence of privilege in another guise. In an authentic articulation of the biblical message, story is gathered up into story, changing what seems changeless. Both the status quo and the existing power structures that sustain it can be unveiled and desacralized. Futurelessness is not immortal; immersion in the present, whether by personal default or institutional constraint, can be overcome. The stories of an open future can suspend those that enable vested interests to condemn the poor to desperation, the oppressed to injustice, the individual to helplessness, and the society at large to callousness. While a new economic order is not equivalent to a "new heaven and a new earth," a biblically envisioned future demands and makes possible nothing less.

Notes

1. Charles R. Strain, "Ideology and Alienation," *Journal of the American Academy of Religion*, December 1977, p. 477.
2. Martin E. Marty, *The Christian Century*, August 2, 1972, p. 795.
3. Robert L. Heilbroner, *Beyond Boom and Crash* (New York: W. W. Norton, 1978), pp. 84–85.
4. John Kenneth Galbraith, *Economics and the Public Purpose* (Boston: Houghton Mifflin, 1973), pp. 81–91.
5. Ibid., pp. 141–45.
6. See Richard R. Nelson, *The Moon and the Ghetto* (New York: W. W. Norton, 1977).
7. Richard Shaull, "Introduction to Paulo Freire," *Pedagogy of the Oppressed* (New York: Seabury, 1973), p. 13.
8. Freire, in Shaull, *Pedagogy of the Oppressed*, p. 34.
9. Theodore Roszak, *The Making of a Counter Culture* (Garden City, N.Y.: Doubleday, Anchor Books, 1969), p. 240.
10. W. Robertson Nicol, *The Expositor's Greek Testament* (Grand Rapids, Mich.: Eerdmans, 1951), pp. 122–23.
11. Alfredo Fierro, *The Militant Gospel* (Maryknoll, N.Y.: Orbis Books, 1977), p. 257.

12. Martin Buber, *Between Man and Man* (London: Routledge and Kegan Paul, 1947), p. 42.

13. Paul Tillich, *The Courage to Be* (New Haven, Conn.: Yale Univ. Press, 1952), p. 89.

14. Peter L. Berger and Thomas Luckmann, *The Social Construction of Reality* (Garden City, N.Y.: Doubleday, Anchor Books, 1967), p. 4.

15. Jürgen Moltmann, *The Church in the Power of the Spirit* (New York: Harper and Row, 1977), p. 225.

16. John Bennett, "Fitting the Liberation Theme into Our Theological Agenda," *Christianity and Crisis,* July 18, 1977, p. 169.

7 The Content of Transcendence

Stories about an open future abound, as do those which lead to futurelessness. What story will hold the future open? For significant change to occur in society we need a story that can never yield to immersion in the present, one that can resist becoming a statement of "what is." A biblically envisioned future is distinguished not only by the category of transcendence but by its content as well. That feature prevents the collapse of a utopia into an accommodation with present arrangements. It allows persons to do more than live in their circumstances; it enables them to rise above and work against a present whose social and economic conditions contract the time and space to be free.

Some stories for their very effectiveness require ambiguity "at the top." American civil religion is a case in point. Specificity would imperil the functionality of the religion. The capacity of the civil religion for integration is inversely related to the particularity of transcendence. In the realm of private faith, there may be a disposition to paint the deity with faint strokes. A God defined is more difficult to restrain and utilize. One's personal story may more readily be told with a deity as a supporting actor.

Some academic theologians have argued that liberation theology is careless about transcendence. One obvious reason is that it does not begin in doctrines. Traditionally, we have had a sense that God was in control if one began in creeds and conventional formulations. Then the situation of humankind in all its temporality would not distort revelation. That ordering of theology has its appeal, but the confidence it yields the more biblical understanding of tran-

174

scendence may be an illusion. The possibility of a cultural captivity is always real, but indifference to context is too high a price to pay for an "immaculate conception." To be contextually conditioned is not tantamount to perversion! "There is no way in which a historical faith (one that has received embodiment in specific times and place) could be expressed other than through the cultural norms and patterns in which it is located. If it did not do so, it would fail to communicate. If it did not do so, it would not be historical."[1] The God who is embedded in human affairs is inevitably embedded in particular ones in a particular time and place. All attempts to write the definitive creed are finally seen to be reflections of the era in which they were written. Freedom from history in the development of theology is as impossible as it is undesirable. Even a systematic theologian like Paul Tillich began in the questions arising out of experience—a particular history.

The doctrine of God is no exception to the stipulation that theology be written from below. Indeed, it is the most essential illustration of the need. It must be significant that a loss of confidence in the discourse about transcendence follows an era in which theologians and preachers worked confidently from within the faith. If nothing else, the momentary enthusiasm for the Death of God movement signaled that professionals had been only communicating with each other, without a point of contact in their constituencies.

Liberation theology will likely never produce a doctrine of God that will appease academic theologians obsessed with the architecture of systems. Nor is that an aspiration of liberation theology. One would have to move away from history and narrative to accomplish an adequate conceptualization. A refined and full-blown statement is not possible when theology is summoned from below. Those who are sensitive to the cry of pain within the situation will detect and accept aspects of the reality of God but will not presume to do more. What may be known about God through Scripture, tradition, and the community of faith, is best invoked by the story in which one is understanding experience. For our time the story of futurelessness is the one in view as one asks about God. We can only authentically speak of God within what is being experienced. That means our story in relation to the story of God will be in fragments, bits and pieces, rather than neat formulations. Liberation theology takes the risk of letting the need of the time sort out and lay claim to aspects of the divine reality.

A. Presence in the Other

The Christian tradition has had a propensity for beginning with a notion of God as Creator, following without imagination or insight the first book of the Old Testament. "Creator of heaven and earth" is a controlling reference point. No wonder generations of youth at religious camps have been taken up to a high mountain for an encounter with God as the sun set slowly in the West and "Taps" was the background for lowering the flag. Then follows a meditation on the theme "God's in his heaven, all's right with the world." The Messiah has his function invoked with a gentle singing of "Fairest Lord Jesus, ruler of all nature." Our ancestors within ancient Israel could not relate to that. Their sense of God was informed by the Exodus experience. They learned to use the divine name in the situation of futurelessness, in the moments when what lay at hand was oppression.

Biblically speaking, where do we find God? Nature has its place, but it yields a cosmic chill as readily as it does the assurance of creation for our benefit and enjoyment. Interpersonal niceties have their place, but there is no evidence that encounter groups are mandated by the aspiration for revelation. The "single one" has his place before an "Eternal Thou," but we come alone to our image of the divine and we are left alone. Rather, it is in the appeal of the "other" that God locates and calls to action: "Only the summons of the poor person, the widow, the orphan, the alien, the crippled constitutes true otherness. Only this summons, accepted and heeded, makes us transcend the sameness and original solitude of the self; only in this summons do we find the transcendence in which God consists."[2] The word of God about God is in the crucibles of existence, in the imperative to respond where futurelessness holds sway. The voice of God is in the man beaten and robbed and left to die, skillfully avoided by all but the despised Samaritan. Access to God is in the neighbor who calls for help and solidarity. Our response to that appeal may be personal as well as impersonal, in relationship or through systemic caring. In his remarkable wisdom, Karl Barth saw that Jesus' commandment to love the neighbor was bifocal—there is the near and distant neighbor.[3] The near neighbor is not only the one at hand but the one for whom we have feelings. We are involved with him, we react and our reactions elicit a response. In some ways this "other" is easiest to love. We are rewarded in the feelings that become operative between us; our efforts may even feed on his response. But the distant neighbor is another matter. That person may or may not be close at hand, more likely not. Emotionally we have no involvement in the individual's well-being. Interpersonal intensity may not even be desirable. This "other" is a real test of our capacity to love because we have to find a way of doing right without the feelings that stimulate interaction. For this person we need, in the words of Earl Warren, "a political conception of compassion." To love the distant "other" is to care through the structures of the social order that restrict or enable the future. "To be meaningful and plausible, the very proclamation that God loves us calls for the mediation of politics, for a practical movement which will alter the existing social situation."[4]

God is known in the cry of pain, in all the anguish that futurelessness engenders. God's voice is the voice of the abandoned and forsaken, God's body is the body of the hungry and naked. God's spirit is the spirit of the imprisoned and tormented. Epiphanies are there before they are anywhere else. Dorothee Söelle explores the story of the man at the pool at Bethesda in John's Gospel, chapter 5, as a model of where the claim falls upon us. The sick man had been lying beside the pool, believing as did others, that entry could mean healing. When Jesus asked, "Do you want to be healed?" he responded, "Sir, I have no man to put me into the pool" (John 5:7). He is alone, helpless, and therefore condemned to futurelessness. He is the "other" without a chance for healing. His situation has a social context. "I have no man. . . ." Alas, "his illness . . . is not his private affair with which he must deal alone; it is brought into a social context which poses a question to other men."[5] Jesus ends that isolation with his word. People are brutalized in social contexts and God sides with the brutalized, appealing to us to be the "man" who lifts the other into a healing position.

The question to which liberation theologians have been indifferent centers on the futurelessness of the oppressors. Can the oppressor be the "other" in whom God locates? It would appear not. Often there is an appeal to a passage from Karl Barth: "God stands at every time unconditionally and passionately on this and only on this side: always against the exalted and for the lowly, always against those who already have rights and for those from whom they are robbed and taken away."[6] The humanity of God is invested in those getting hurt and the weight of the divine presence is with their need. Indeed, in the contest at hand it could not be otherwise. Between the one who imposes futurelessness and the one upon whom it is imposed, there could be no other alignment. But what is overlooked is that at some level the victors are victims; while not oppressed, they are caught in the role of oppressor. The obligation to love the neighbor includes all victims. Fierro quotes Girardi to the point: "One loves the oppressed by liberating them from their misery; one loves the oppressors by liberating them from their sinfulness."[7] That need not mean that the oppressed are without sin and the oppressors without misery. But it is a statement that God can locate in the need of both the oppressed and the oppressor and calls us in the plight of each. There is more than one story of futurelessness. While God sides with the cause of the oppressed, that does not preclude God's presence to the oppressors; they must be freed from the oppression they create. No one is excluded from the possibility of being the "other" in whom the summons of God is present.

B. Participation in Suffering

Futurelessness has degrees of intensity. There are obvious differences between the experience of the oppressed and the oppressors. While both may be trapped, the difference between them is marked by suffering. Theology of liberation has an obsession with that phenomenon which no broadening of the base of futurelessness can dilute. The relentless agenda of liberation theology is working on "the abolition of circumstances under which people are forced to suffer."[8] There is, of course, a distinction to be made between suffering which can be brought to an end and that which is an inevitable consequence of existence. We cheapen the quality of existence if we promote the illusion that all suffering is to be eliminated or avoided. One need not move to the rather perverse claim that suffering produces character—and is therefore good for us—to affirm it as a natural constituent in existence. But it is what is not inevitable that concerns us.

Suffering is a battered wife whose husband vents the frustrations of unemployment on her. Suffering is Auschwitz and six million Jews who were the victims of a perverse movement and the inertia of the masses. It is confinement to a stereotype that lowers self-worth and precludes the exercise of capabilities. Suffering is having a foreign country for unknown reasons spray napalm on your children, enter the village of My Lai sharing bullets as if they were jelly beans, and watch indifferently while the courageous are confined to tiger cages. It is being the victim of a disease that vaccination could prevent if you knew about it and could afford it. Suffering is being a laborer who has no leverage against the corporation, the economic system, and the society at large with which to gain tolerable conditions and wages proportionate to need. Suffering is silence brought on by the fear of recrimination and the internal revulsion with which one has learned to live. Suffering is having so little self-regard that you turn on yourself and your environment in contempt. It is a father and mother watching the object of their love wither for want of nourishment or medication. Suffering is having become so submissive that one's only identity is derived from others. Suffering is when suffering has become so normal one no longer thinks of it as unnatural.

It is only with suffering in view—in this instance, that suffering we can end by changing the order of society—that we may dare to speak of God. For generations the best that theologians could produce was a pious, "God knows your pain and cares." It's a short stroll from that to the doctor in Camus's *The Plague* who said he could not believe in a god who let children suffer. Is God apathetic? Or is God, in the words of Woody Allen, an "underachiever"? The custodians of sacred tradition have been reluctant to allow suffering into the experience God experiences. It's as if we could think better of God for that.

The message of the cross is stark and clear. God elects to penetrate our suffering; God is immanent in pain and therefore involved personally in all our anguish. Through Jesus we understand the total identification of God with all dimensions of human suffering. The unambiguous testimony of Scripture points to pain, beatings, exhaustion, hunger, homelessness, desertion, death, even forsakenness by God. Our experience demands and Scripture warrants that we allow our imagination to encompass a suffering God. In order to make that contemporary, both Dorothee Söelle and Jürgen Moltmann appeal to a story told by Elie Wiesel, a survivor of Auschwitz. "The SS hung Jewish men and a boy before the assembled inhabitants of the camp. The men died quickly but the death struggle of the boy lasted half an

hour. 'Where is God? Where is he?' a man behind me
asked. As the boy, after a long time, was still in agony on
the rope, I heard the man cry again, 'Where is God now'
and I heard a voice within me answer, 'Here he is—he is
hanging here on this gallows.' "[9]
The strange logic of our faith is that Christ is a battered
woman, an Auschwitz Jew, a Vietnamese child, the victim
of a preventable disease, a laborer who lost human agency
on the job, a victim intimidated into silence, one in whom
self-contempt has taken over, a helpless parent, a person
who has come to accept his suffering as the norm—"here he
is—he is hanging here on this gallows."
The immersion of God in the pain that could be brought
to an end makes the situation different. God's sharing the
suffering alters the notion that suffering is meant to be. The
involvement of God as victim creates the possibility that
the way things are today need not be. Part of that, of
course, is in the faith that Easter is on the far side of Good
Friday; the victim becomes victor. With God as participant
in suffering, there is a restoration of nerve and an incite-
ment to action. Our silence, submission, and acceptance
yield; revulsion and revolt hold sway. The suffering God
creates a sense that the present need not be the way it is.
Altering the rhetoric of another decade: "the present has
been canceled." The world in fact can change. From within
the pain the conviction takes hold that one can emerge from
an existence as an object and become a "single one" again.
And from the sidelines the stakes are raised immeasurably
higher when one knows who is suffering on the gallows.
The suffering God is a claim to action, an invitation to
serve the pain of God in the other and in our history. Sen-
sitization to that pain which God embraces leads one to
participation. One is set at the point of decision. There is no
innocence and there is no possibility of neutrality. The decision in the face of suffering is a decision for or against God.
Dorothee Söelle quotes Thomas Muntzer as saying in his
manifesto to miners at Allstedt, "If you don't want to suffer
for the sake of God, then you must become the devil's

martyrs."[10] While his injunction was to the peasants who accepted their exploitation, it reaches just as forcefully to those who view the futurelessness from the sidelines. In the context of suffering, atheism has a new meaning. It is not the denial of God's existence but the refusal to share in the suffering of God in our history. The awesome message of the New Testament is that the God fully present in our world waits between Good Friday and Easter morning for us to act against whatever oppresses, systemically or personally, the "others" in whom the deity locates. The suffering God waits!

C. God's Glory and Justice

In any reflection upon the human condition one inevitably comes to the issue of justice. But each person's perspective determines what coming to justice really means. At the level of abstraction, *justice* is a neutral term that can be managed skillfully in relation to love and power. Most discussions begin "from above" with speculative explorations into the distribution of scarce resources, the formulation and application of the law, or principles that embody the claims of love. Those considerations have their place, but not in liberation theology. We come to justice from the experience of suffering, either our own or in identification with the suffering of others. Then justice is not a problem— it is a person in pain. And the thrust of justice is to abolish forces and systems that inflict suffering. Justice concerns itself with conditions that can and must be changed. It is a mandate to eliminate the causes of pain.

The God who locates in "the others" needing help and solidarity, who is immanent in human suffering, gives the phenomenon new dimension. God's own reality is at issue. What beginning from below teases out is the relation of justice to God. José Miranda documents the contention that "the glory of God" and "the justice of God" are synonymous.[11] Justice is the controlling manifestation. A number of texts explicitly juxtapose glory and justice.

The peoples will see your justice, and all the kings your glory. (Isaiah 62:2a)

The heavens proclaim his justice, and all the peoples his glory. (Psalms 97:6)

To praise God for his justice, the most high for his glory. (Qumran)

Other texts relate God's glory to dwelling on earth in "compassion, goodness, peace, and above all justice."[12] In the third chapter of Romans, Paul develops the need of Jew and Gentile for the glory of God. The glory of God is in reality a new era in which justice reigns. It is to be something that permeates the earth. The Gospel of John collates with these themes in articulating the meaning of the Word becoming flesh: "And we saw his glory, the glory that is his as the only Son of the Father, a glory full of compassion and goodness" (John 1:14). The sense of God's glory as goodness is evident in other passages.

The richness of his glory on the recipients of compassion. (Romans 9:23)

The richness of his grace in goodness . . . (Eph. 2:7)

My God will fulfill all your needs according to his richness in Glory in Christ Jesus. (Phil. 4:19)

Justice is not an attribute of God about which speculative formulations are appropriate; it is a manifestation of a presence in the midst of suffering.

The consequence of this is that knowing God and doing justice have an intimate relationship. A text from Jeremiah (chapter 22) exposes the connection. Josiah and Jehoiakim were kings of Israel ruling in succession, but their similarities ended with familial ties. Josiah's conduct as king was marked by concern for the poor and deprived in his realm. That is not to suggest he embraced for himself the conditions of poverty. Indeed, he "enjoyed the material comforts of kingly office." Yet the fact that Josiah lived well did not make him indifferent to those who did not.[13] His son had another view of his regal rights. At a critical time in the life of Israel he proceeded to construct a luxurious palace on Mt. Zion. It was "built by forced labor, with callous disregard for the rights of wage earners, and lavishly decorated" in a manner befitting an oriental despot.[14] Jeremiah was incensed, and his indignation found expression in an oracle: "Woe to him who builds his house by unrighteousness, and his upper rooms by injustice, who makes his neighbors serve him for nothing, and does not give him his wages." Then he asked one of those question in which the answer is already given: "Do you think you are a king because you compete in cedar?" In other words, do you think sumptuous surroundings make you regal? Without waiting for an answer, Jeremiah invoked the comparison with Jehoiakim's father. "He judged the cause of the poor and the needy, then it was well. Is not this to know me? says the Lord." To know God is to take up the "cause of the poor and needy." Knowing God and doing justice are correlates.

Some, of course, might want to invert the formula. Could we not say that to do justice is to know God? In most instances equations can be read forward and backward. The New Testament comes close to warranting that. One might think of passages in John which suggest that one who abides in love abides in God, for God is love. Then the floodgates are open; anyone who is loving and caring by virtue of deeds is in relation to God—whether aware of it or not. Now if we work the formula both forward and backward we have an interesting problem. Those who profess to know God—but do not do justice—don't really know God. And those who profess not to know God—but do justice— know God whether they realize it or not.

But if we are more careful, and more faithful to the text, we see that the formula does not invert. When one claims, "to know God is to do justice," there is a hidden clause. Jeremiah makes the point explicitly in another text: "Thus says the Lord, 'Let not the wise man glory in his wisdom, let not the mighty man glory in his might, let not the rich man glory in his riches; but let him who glories glory in this; that he understands and knows me, that I am the Lord who practices love, justice and righteousness in the earth; for in these things I delight,' says the Lord." There is a connection established between knowing God and doing justice which alters the simple equation. God's "character" becomes the norm: "to know the Lord is to pattern one's life after God's own action."[15] When we know God we do justice—because that is what God does. God reveals his glory in acts of justice. The person who knows God participates in what God is doing in human history. Those who fail to embrace "the cause of the poor and the needy" do not know God. Whether one recalls the Exodus and the delivery of the Israelites from bondage in Egypt or the life and ministry of Jesus, God comes in where persons are getting hurt. God invades and is involved in the injustices of the human realm. What is astonishing is that God sides with the little people, those who seem to have no levers with which to overcome their suffering. The Bible takes the awesome risk of confusing the Creator with creation. That risk peaks in Jesus of Nazareth. He makes the human condition so conspicuously his own that we can name him in our suffering.

Some years ago, a Protestant church on Chicago's near west side—a blighted area by any standard—was responsible for creating a slum litany. While some may dismiss it as too shocking and others dismiss it for its theological shortcomings, it makes a point too near the biblical record to be ignored:

> O God, who lives in tenements, who goes to
> segregated schools, who is beaten in precincts,
> who is unemployed,
> O God, who hangs on street corners, who tastes the
> grace of cheap wine and the sting of needles,
> O God, who is pregnant without husband, who is child
> without parent, who has no place to play,

O God, who can't read nor write, who is on
welfare and who is treated like garbage,
O God, whose name is spick, black nigger, bastard,
guinea and kike,
O God, who smells and has no place to bathe . . .

And the refrain of the congregation is "help us to know you
. . . to touch you . . . to see you . . . to be with you." To
know God is to do justice. The divine is present in the hurts
and pain, deprivations and perversions, ugliness and emp-
tiness of our world. The person who really knows God
recognizes and is drawn into the action uniquely God's. "I
am the Lord who practices love, justice, and righteousness." We receive the Lord in our responses to the claims
laid upon us by "the other" who suffers. Then, "transcendence does not mean only an unimaginable and inconceivable God, but a God who is accessible only in the acts
of justice."[16]

D. Relinquishment and the Ineffable

The presence of God "in the act of justice" will mean
relief for many, but for most of us it means relinquishment.
The alleviation of suffering by attacking the forces and systems that perpetuate it requires a yielding of power and
privilege. The God who locates in "the other" confronts us
with the obligation to forsake our advantages. In a finite
universe, for the "have-nots" to "have," those who "have"
must "have not" in some significant degree. Our possessions and powers are at the expense of the deprivation and
exploitation of others. Obviously, there is no way to redress the imbalance without substantial and painful relinquishment. Instinctively, we understand that within a family unit parents may readily sacrifice in order for their child
to have an opportunity. For the most part, we do not
transpose that logic to larger units, including the world family. The prevailing assumption is that others can be brought

up to where we are through a mix of economic growth and the wonders of technology. Historically, that mix has increased disparity. The system that creates injustice has not been altered.

Relinquishment means we cannot count as our own what we think we and others deserve; it means the instruments of decision and distribution cannot remain under our domination. Relinquishment is the most difficult demand that love makes upon us, and not only because the claim is usually from the "distant neighbors" where interpersonal forces such as those within the family are not in play. The radicality is evident in that it obligates us to amputate expressions of our identity. Who we are and what we can do is intertwined with our privilege, power, and possessions. The claim for relinquishment, then, calls for us to let go of those things through which we know and name ourselves. When a substantial ego investment has occurred, any act of divestiture is costly and painful for the human personality.

The recognition that God's glory is in doing justice means that victory is in the "materiality of creation." There is only a "bodily glory," as Karl Barth expressed it in his commentary on Romans (see discussion of Romans 8:19–22). In Barth's blunt terms, "to overlook suffering is to overlook Christ."[17] In the measure that suffering can be alleviated, it usually involves a release on our part of things we have come to value. While those who suffer come to God in and with their anguish and find God in suffering identification, the rest of us come to God as thieves and find our Lord in the imperative to relinquish. But alas, bold claims by themselves do not carry with them the possibility of their enactment. Relinquishment as a new form of law is a barrier to fulfillment. What in the understanding of God can enable our "passage" to freedom from our dependence on power, possessions, and privilege?

The need for psychological liberation, and its relation to transcendence, is much more subtle and complex than political liberation. We are led into realms where it is more difficult to speak, where words trail off into strident inadequacy. Nothing in the Exodus model serves us in the move from possessiveness to indebtedness, from protecting to sharing our rights and resources. Abraham Heschel, whose impact was as intense as any in the political realm, leads us into a consideration of the "ineffable" as the predicate for personal transformation.[18] The ineffable is that which lies beyond our grasp, yet "inhabits the magnificent and the common, the grandiose and the tiny facts of reality alike."[19] It is an apprehension of the world in which we recognize that we are not so acquainted with it as we first thought. The sublime experiences are always ones in which we become aware that what is "really there" is beyond our grasp. There is a presence permeating all reality which provokes feelings of awe and wonder. It is the intuition that the universe is charged with a grandeur not of our making and resistant to our control. "The practical mind pays more attention to the commas and colons in the great text of reality than to its content and meaning. While to the sense of the ineffable things stand out like marks of exclamation, like silent witnesses . . . all things carry a surplus of meaning. . . . It is as if all things were vibrant with spiritual meaning, and all we try to do in creative art and in good deeds is to intone the secret strain, an aspect of that meaning."[20] The ineffable is experienced as that which surpasses what we routinely experience and calls us into an awareness of the "beyond in our midst." The word *God* properly occurs when we need to name the quality of wonder, the sense of the ineffable in the known world. It is our symbol for the sense of a spiritual presence in our materiality.

What the experience of the ineffable does is to intercept a division of all things into sacred and profane spheres and the ordering of our lives accordingly. There is no profane independent of the sacred and no sacred outside the profane. Wonder and awe have no categories of their own. "The "spiritual presence" is not acosmic. There is only a "bodily glory." We come to the "divine aspect of the universe" from a sense of the ineffable and with an awareness that all we handle with our minds and hands is impregnated.[21] The experience of transcendence is, then, one of being both drawn towards and put off our common course. The wonder experienced creates a tension in which the common becomes uncommon and the uncommon becomes common. We want both more and less at the same time. The sublime is attractive and foreboding, appealing and threatening.

The possibility of passage from finding our identity in the powers, possessions, and privileges we have to a freedom from our need for them begins in the experience of the ineffable. Relinquishment may take place when what we have is permeated by a "spiritual presence." It comes as gift, not accomplishment, it ends the need for achievement and success and it breaks the merciless cycles of arrogance and callousness. The response of wonder is transforming in our apprehension of the universe. We cannot hold and behold it in the same way. "Endless wonder unlocks an innate sense of indebtedness. Within our awe there is no place for self-assertion. Within our awe we only know that all we own we owe. The world consists, not of things, but of tasks. Wonder is the state of our being asked. The ineffable is a question addressed to us."[22]

Our psychological transformation occurs in the recognition that "all we own we owe." Rights and resources are not possessions but instruments for sharing. What is intercepted is the very process of intertwining our identity with our possessions, power, and privileges. The universe is on loan—any acts of possession are acts of thievery. Sharing can come about when we learn that our identity is in relation to the "spiritual presence" and not that through which it is mediated. The prospect of "letting go" is created in the recognition that whatever we have in our possession is a gift *and* a claim upon us.

Liberation theology is committed to speaking of God from within the conditions of human anguish and entrapment. That does not fashion an identity of imprecision or ambiguity as civil religion prefers. The contours of God begin to form around a presence in the neighbor, participation in human suffering, the imperatives of doing justice, and the claims of relinquishment. That creates intensity in our theological perspectives, and it may have awesome impact upon our economic structures.

Notes

1. Robert McAfee Brown, "The Rootedness of All Theology," *Christianity and Crisis,* July 18, 1977, p. 170.

2. José Miranda, *Being and the Messiah* (Maryknoll, N.Y.: Orbis Books, 1977), p. 37.

3. Karl Barth, *Church Dogmatics,* vol. 3, part 4 (Edinburgh: T. & T. Clark, 1961), pp. 285–323.

4. Alfredo Fierro, *The Militant Gospel* (Maryknoll, N.Y.: Orbis Books, 1977), p. 74.

5. Dorothee Söelle, *Political Theology* (Philadelphia: Fortress Press, 1974), p. 68.

6. Quoted by George Hunsinger, "Toward a Radical Barth" in *Karl Barth and Radical Politics,* edited and translated by Hunsinger (Philadelphia: Westminster Press, 1976), p. 225.

7. Fierro, *The Militant Gospel,* p. 232.

8. Dorothee Söelle, *Suffering* (Philadelphia: Fortress Press, 1975), p. 2.

9. Elie Wiesel, *Night* (New York: Hill and Wang, 1960), pp. 70–71.

10. Söelle, *Suffering,* p. 133.

11. José Miranda, *Marx and the Bible* (Maryknoll, N.Y.: Orbis Books, 1974), pp. 233–37.

12. Ibid., p. 234.

13. *The Interpreter's Bible,* vol. 5 (Nashville, Tenn.: Abingdon Press, 1956), p. 984.

14. John Skinner, *Prophecy and Religion* (New York: Cambridge Univ. Press, 1951), p. 247.

15. José Miguez Bonino, *Christians and Marxists* (Grand Rapids, Mich.: Eerdmans, 1976), p. 33.

16. Miranda, *Marx and the Bible,* p. 48.

17. Karl Barth, *The Epistle to the Romans* (Fair Lawn, N.J.: Oxford Univ. Press, 1953), p. 305.

18. Abraham Heschel, *Man Is Not Alone* (New York: Farrar, Straus, and Young, 1951).

19. Ibid., p. 5.

20. Ibid., pp. 40–41.

21. Ibid., p. 67.

22. Ibid., p. 69.

8 The Liberation Agenda and the Economic Order

The transfiguration story calls for the creation of a world in which the Eli Blacks can live, a world where the stories in which we live heal rather than tear apart our lives. As that world struggles to be born against the entrenchment of the existing order, the future begins to give shape and substance to the present. The God who shares in the suffering of the world, and indeed is a suffering God, lends the new age its prospect of enactment. God journeys within the journey toward freedom and participates in "the breaking in and breaking up" of the impediments to human fulfillment. God cancels the sacralizing force of American civil religion and the entrapment of the neoclassical story. The new age needs a new economic order.

In the existing economic order, suffering arises because institutional arrangements function to maintain inequitable distributions of jobs, income, wealth, and power. Belief in the neoclassical story leads us to see the economic system as benign and suffering as the result of personal failure; it blinds us to the inequities. However, if we reject that story and begin to tell the true story about the sources of suffering, that in itself does not provide a new economic order. Is it inevitable that the prevailing economic order will create conditions that cause pain? If so, how can that pain be removed? By systemic modification? By revolution? What kinds of changes are necessary and sufficient to remove or neutralize the structural causes of suffering?

191

A. Systemic Modification

In recent years, several powerful constituencies have arisen to criticize and, at the same time, defend the economic system in the United States. They recognize the mismatch between the message of the neoclassical story and the reality of the economic system; they also believe that the system does many things so well that it must be preserved. Their solutions call for changing some features of the prevailing order, but leaving its essence alone. Conservatives see the problems of monopoly power and misallocation of resources as fundamentally caused by too much government regulation. In their view, if regulation were drastically reduced or eliminated, then the natural competitive forces operating in the system could come to the fore and serve societal welfare. They point to the successful deregulation of the airline industry and the supply problems in the energy industry as examples to support this case.[1] One flaw in their argument from the perspective of human need is that even a rigidly competitive system will do little to adjust the current distributions of jobs, income, wealth, and power, and these are the fruits that foster and extend dehumanization. In addition, much of the present noncompetitive structure of large bureaucratic corporations in the productive sphere came into being long before the current era of extensive government regulation. For example, the steel and auto industries reached their present status under conditions of virtually no regulation. It is difficult to see how a total end to regulation would achieve much in terms of creating competitive forces in those industries. The conservative critics may well confuse the superior allocative properties of the market with the full range of benefits supposedly provided by competition.

The liberal reformers, because they do recognize the inherent problems of monopoly and oligopoly power in the American economic system, provide a stronger argument for modification and preservation of that system. Galbraith's analysis is typical of this position. Indeed, he provides much of the thrust for the argument about the inevitable bureaucratization of the economy. He believes that in the prevailing economic order, large corporations, government, and large labor unions lie outside the effective control of markets. Further, the nature of the "planning system" is such that all three types of bureaucracies often work together to achieve goals that are significantly at variance with societal welfare.[2]

Galbraith contends, however, that the problems caused by these structures can be alleviated without dismantling the entire system. The productive bureaucracies should not be eliminated because their size has allowed them to create reasonably low-cost production technologies. These are not often used at peak efficiency, but they still keep costs of production below what would prevail if those industries were dominated by many smaller producers. The government and labor bureaucracies have arisen partly in self-defense against the excessive power of the productive bureaucracies. It is this latter growth that Galbraith sees as the beginning of a solution to the problem of making the system serve social need. He calls for further and more carefuly directed growth of other large institutions which could then become "countervailing powers" to balance against the existing structures. As an example, a large monopolistic corporation within a particular labor market will have some real control over the demand for labor in that market. It will be able to influence significantly the wage rate and/or the hours worked. In fact, it was precisely because of such control that labor unions first began to emerge. A large union with some monopoly control over the supply of labor can counter the impact of the monopoly employer.

Galbraith would like to expand this notion so that there might be several countervailing powers operating within a particular part of the economic system. He believes that such an arrangement could serve as an effective substitute for the market and approximate the service of societal welfare that the market fails to provide. He is particularly enamored of the potential role for the government in both regulation and planning.

Historically, regulation has not served its avowed purposes very well. It is too easy for regulatory bodies to be captured by the industry ostensibly being regulated. It takes an expert to regulate an industry properly; one gets to be an expert by being part of the industry. The regulatory experts begin with an inherent bias that favors the industry.[3] It is not clear how Galbraith's countervailing powers can overcome the problem—good intentions are not enough.

According to Galbraith, much of the economic activity in the United States is already planned. That is normal behavior for the large bureaucratic productive organizations that comprise the planning system. What he is calling for is a formalization of the process with an overall national plan into which the private sector plans must fit.[4] The national planning goals would be designed to pursue societal welfare. Insofar as the federal government and the national planning authority were able to exercise a countervailing influence on actual economic behavior, the potentially negative impacts of the plans of the private productive bureaucracies would be mitigated. This seems more promising than the regulatory approach, but it is not clear who will control the national planning bureaucracy. It is too easy for a symbiotic relationship to develop between the various levels of planning. There is a very strong temptation to serve their own and each others' interests and to ignore the common good. For example, Soviet planners have responded to certain special interests and overexpanded their defense industries. This has made it virtually impossible to service effectively the growing needs of consumers.

James Kuhn has modified Galbraith's ideas by suggesting that the source of the difficulties comes from the nature of the decision-making process itself.[5] Since business decisions are made in terms of goals like profit, risk spreading, expansion, and job security, it is not surprising that they make decisions that reflect those concerns and ignore broader social issues. Kuhn wants to involve other interested and affected persons and organizations in business decisions that go beyond the interests of the firm itself. To some extent, current processes do that. For example, when a power company wants to build a new generating plant, it must first makes its own decisions about the size, location, fuel source, and economic viability of the project. Then the various public utility commissions, Federal Power Commission, and Department of Energy hold hearings and cause the decisions to be modified. Next, the various environmental agencies make their input, followed by zoning and development commissions and concerned citizens. But all of this occurs serially and is tremendously wasteful of time as well as human and other productive resources.

Kuhn suggests that all of the interested parties be involved in the power company's initial decision. In that way, the decision reflects not only the economic considerations germane to the firm's interests, but also the positive and negative externalities that will have an impact on the society at large. Implementation would require some method for creating and granting power to interested parties; they must be able to affect the decision, to force the decision-making process to be responsive to them. Various formal regulatory agencies have legal authority and can use it to help shape decisions, but Kuhn envisions something broader than that. How could we effectively involve an organization like the Sierra Club or an individual like Ralph Nader, who have no formal sources of power, in decisions that affect their vision of social need? One suggestion is that all interested parties be granted some political "chips" which they could choose to expend to influence various decisions. The Sierra Club could use all of its chips to affect one major environmental issue, or it could spread them out to influence a number of decisions. The idea is intriguing, although the task of setting up such a system and deciding who gets how many chips would be monumental.

Both Galbraith and Kuhn are attempting to modify the

existing system in order to eliminate its worst effects on social welfare while retaining its essential features. Their ideas are very useful and may constitute desirable first steps in the necessary process of social change. They ultimately fail to respond to the basic issue of removing structures and eliminating circumstances that create suffering and oppression. The sources of denial of human freedom are systemic and structural. The solutions Kuhn and Galbraith propose do not involve removal of the offending institutions but the creation of new institutions to control the old ones. There is no doubt that effective counteraction of existing social conditions will require construction of new institutions to challenge the entrenched vested interests. The liberation agenda, however, demands much more than that.

Creating the time and space for freedom, firmly establishing human agency, and assuring subject status for all are some of the goals that must energize the new economic order. Counter-institutions may help to eliminate some of the conditions that create pain and futurelessness, but they cannot create conditions that ensure fulfillment of the goals. Such institutions will eventually become, in Veblen's words, "unseasonable," and they too will begin to impede the full development of human freedom.[6] It is perhaps paradoxical that new structures are necessary to deal with current problems, but they cannot ultimately provide "solutions" that ensure freedom. The assumption that new structural mechanisms are enough perpetuates futurelessness; it precludes real alternatives.

Therefore, systemic modifications a la Galbraith or Kuhn, while they may be first steps, must finally give way to more fundamental change. The goals must be separated from the institutions that serve them. While institutions are indispensable, they should be created *and* dismantled in relation to human need. The liberation agenda calls for the journey toward freedom, not the construction of institutions, to be the center of analysis and action.

When the focus does switch to the human condition, new

values begin to emerge that require different models and call for different stories. Within the economic sphere the neoclassical model and its associated stories with their emphasis on self-interest must give way to the agenda of the liberation story. This story has its emphasis firmly centered on the common good, on human need, and on human freedom. There are many features of the prevailing order that impede the emergence of the new story. The most powerful of these are the drive to accumulate with the associated property rights of the accumulator, and the tendency toward bureaucratic organization in the economic realm. It is these facets of the existing order that place the greatest pressure on human freedom. They create conditions that give rise to suffering and oppression.

B. The Drive to Accumulate

There is one aspect of a market system that is continually glossed over in the presentation of neoclassical economic models and effectively hidden from view by the dominance of the competitive neoclassical story. A natural outgrowth of the pursuit of self-interest is the accumulation of the profits from the production process. The neoclassical story has convinced many in the society that such accumulation either is unlikely because competition will force profit to zero, or is of positive benefit because the pursuit of profit will lead to efficient use of resources.

In reality, accumulation is not unlikely and its benefits may be far from positive. There is little evidence to suggest that either individuals or corporations use accumulated wealth in ways that consistently benefit society. Their pursuit of self-interest is exactly that—pursuit of self-interest. The absence of perfect competition vitiates Adam Smith's "invisible hand" so that societal welfare is served only accidentally, if at all, by the prevailing economic order.

This argument need not be telescoped into assertions; it

has analytic validity. It is the competitive drive that attracts new entrants into an industry and forces productive reinvestment of profit. The same competitive drive assures that all producers of a particular product will strive for efficiency and will all eventually find the same "best" combination of resources and technology. Competition for customers will force prices down to the minimum level consistent with costs, and eliminate long-run economic profit. Without profit in the long run, there is no source for excessive accumulation.

In the United States, as in other industrial societies, the conditions for perfect competition do not exist and accumulation has occurred. Both individuals and corporations have amassed wealth and this has enabled them to skew the distribution of income in their favor. Only a small fraction of all income recipients are able to receive significant amounts of income from property and other accumulated wealth. The ownership of wealth and wealth-generated income confers much more economic power on the wealth holders than on those whose only source of income is the sale of their own labor services. Economic power includes command over productive activity. The ownership of the means of production vested in individuals, and more particularly in corporations, ensures them of some control over what gets produced. The income generated by their ownership gives them more dollar votes as consumers, further extending their ability to control production.

How has accumulation occurred to such an extent in an economic system whose ostensible competitiveness ought to have prevented the amassing of large amounts of wealth? In the first instance, economies of scale and markets large enough to accommodate only a few producers violated the perfect competition paradigm and led to producers that were large relative to their markets. The resulting market control allowed economic profit to persist in the long run and created the opportunity for accumulation to occur. More generally, the benefits of technology were not readily dispersed to all producers but were jealously guarded by both patent rights and merger. One producer *could* maintain an advantage for a long period of time, grow large relative to other producers and the market, gain some degree of market control, and thus accumulate long-run economic profit.

Once economic profit was changed from a signal for movement of competitive forces into a normal condition, large business was freed from the constant pressure to operate efficiently in order to maximize profit. Some degree of profitability in the long run was virtually assured by the market control created by accumulated wealth. The firm was free to pursue other goals such as growth and sales expansion, vertical and/or horizontal integration, or extensive development of new product lines. None of these goals is, in itself, symbolic of evil action or intent on the part of a business corporation, but they certainly do not involve the same efficient utilization of resources that would occur with the single-minded pursuit of profit in a competitive world. While efficient use of resources is not the only factor contributing to welfare, when resources are used inefficiently, societal welfare is reduced

Accumulation is an important part of the material advance in any industrial economic system. Economic growth in such systems depends upon and is driven by investment to create more productive capacity. Investment comes out of accumulated surplus. That is, the system produces more than it needs to consume during a given period and the excess is used to create more productive capacity for the future. In a capitalist free-enterprise society, that productive capacity is owned by individuals or corporations and confers wealth, status, and most particularly, economic power, upon them.

No one wants to sacrifice the economic growth or impair the material advance that is an integral part of industrial development. Unfortunately, in all industrial societies, accumulated wealth and productive capacity have been used to confer and increase the status and power of certain groups. There is no doubt that the general level of material well-being is significantly greater in such industrial societies than in nonindustrial ones. Because of the power conferred by accumulated wealth, however, the distribution of that well-being tends to be skewed heavily toward the controllers of wealth. More significantly, wealthy individuals, corporations, and power groups are able to use their control over wealth to make the economic system serve their interests.

One important feature of the liberation agenda is the commitment to relinquishment—"all that we own we owe." To be faithful to that agenda, accumulated wealth must be made to serve the society at large, not special interest groups. The existing wealth-controlling institutions have been established around a private property ethic that positively encourages using wealth to serve self-interest. Despite the claims of the revisionists, such institutions cannot be reshaped to serve the common good. The move from self-interest to "all that we own we owe" is too wrenching for the fabric of those institutions to be sustained. The short-range goal must include the elimination of those institutions and their replacement with others that will use wealth to serve the broad interests of society. The first steps in that replacement should include a tax on accumulated wealth, limitations on the property rights of corporations, and broader involvement of labor and the public in production and investment decisions. Since all institutions carry the seeds of vested interest, it is also necessary to keep the long-range goal of human freedom, enhanced by relinquishment, firmly in the center of the vision. The means by which change can occur will be addressed more extensively in the last section of this chapter.

C. The Bureaucratization of Power

In any industrial society, control over the use of wealth resides largely with certain corporate or government bureaucracies. Earlier it was established that bureaucratic decision making leads to immersion in the present. It is important to realize that such development seems to be a normal and invariable occurrence whenever industrialization reaches a certain stage. While that cannot be prevented, the question remains, can it be effectively controlled? Bureaucracies are institutions that arise to serve the needs of those in power. The growth of bureaucracy enhances their position in the measure they are able to use the bureaucracy effectively. Ultimately, however, the bureaucracy itself gains the power and uses it to serve its own needs.[7] That raises two fundamental issues that must be addressed if there is to be any hope of breaking the domination that subordinates human need to the interests of the bureaucratic elite.

The first issue concerns the transfer of power from the hands of the few to those of the many. The existing distribution of jobs, income, wealth, and power clearly intercepts the aspirations of women, blacks, and other nonwhite minorities, denies them human agency, and severely limits or removes their control over their own destinies. It negates their own story and forces them to live in a story permeated by the competitive neoclassical model. This eliminates any access to power and leaves them with no systematic way to challenge the bureaucratic structures that dominate their lives.

Economic power is one pole around which bureaucracy forms. Is there some way to reallocate that power so that as new bureaucratic structures form they represent something more than the needs of the old power structure? Under current conditions, blacks are unlikely to gain any real power in the existing corporate bureaucracy because they have neither the income nor the accumulated wealth to buy a place. Furthermore, historical patterns of discrimination in education have left few blacks with the skills required to win a place in the management elite that directs the production activity. This creates a vicious circle: lacking power, they cannot gain position; lacking position, they cannot gain power.

Even if there were some way to redistribute power equally to all members of society, bureaucratic structures would not disappear. But as new bureaucracies arose, they would have a broader base and would serve the interests of a wider spectrum of society. The thrust of the solutions proposed by Galbraith and Kuhn is toward a reorientation of bureaucracy. They are confident that with some modification of existing structures a radical redistribution of power will occur. Other critics see no hope for restructuring "bent" institutions. They opt for the more radical suggestion of a direct redistribution of wealth and income, confident that if the source of power is redistributed, the institutions will be forced to follow.[8]

Any useful solution must deal with both power and institutions—they are separable but interrelated. If institutions are reoriented but wealth and income are not redistributed, the structures will quickly revert to the service of vested interest. If income and wealth are redistributed without institutional restructuring, economic power will reaccumulate in the hands of a few. As a result, only proposals that call for both can achieve any lasting change.

The second issue is the one of recognizing those structures that need to be torn down or changed. Since all bureaucracies will serve their own interests, how does one decide that a particular institution has become so self-serving that the broader goals of society have been too extensively subverted? When is it time to modify or destroy an existing institution?

It might be tempting to perform radical surgery and eliminate most of the existing economic institutions. However, certain structures have a greater power than others to affect our lives and subjugate our personhood. It is important to direct effort at those places where it will have the most effect. The most bureaucratized institutions are the ones that are the most dehumanizing. Their concentration on their own internal logic and needs makes them unable to respond effectively to the broader human needs of society. The institutions that now have the greatest power to limit and control human lives and restrict human freedom are the largest corporate, financial, and government bureaucracies. Their power is directly related to their ability to control economic action, and that is determinzed by size. Control of their power begins by limiting their growth. In addition, restructuring can place their power at the service of human need.

Restrictions on the property rights of corporate and financial institutions in order to limit their ability to accumulate and their right to merge would begin to restrain their growth. Transfer of ownership and management rights into the hands of workers and the public would begin to reorient their interests toward societal rather than bureaucratic needs. The power of government bureaucracies should also be limited and redirected. These structural changes are fundamental and far-reaching. Accomplishing them while firmly maintaining the centrality of the liberation agenda will require enormous effort.

The liberation story calls for a new economic order. Modifying the existing system without fundamentally changing the uses of accumulated wealth and bureaucratic power will not create that new order. New economic priorities that displace self-interest must come to the fore so that wealth and power are used in response to human need and to enhance human freedom.

D. Reordering the Economic Priorities

The issues in this section can be focused by asking two questions: How can we organize the economic activity of an industrial society so that the accumulation necessary to foster growth does not lead to an inequitable distribution of wealth and power? How can we gain the risk-spreading and cost-reducing benefits of economic expansion without development of self-serving bureaucratic structures?

In the economic sphere, the creation of a system that serves human need and promotes justice and human freedom pivots on at least three issues. The first is increasing the range of real choice for individuals. The second is the development of nonexploitive production mechanisms. And the third is a distribution system responsive to human need.

The issue of choice arises because this is a world of scarcity. For most resources, goods, and services, demand would be greater than available supply if the price were zero. We cannot have everything we want or need; we must choose among mutually exclusive alternatives. If the limitations upon available resources, the distribution system, or the organization of production create an environment where no choice is possible, then there is no human freedom.[9] Therefore, one aspect involved in enhancing human freedom is the expansion of the range of choices available to the individual and the society.

Markets can and do serve private choice, but that cannot dominate the vision. Market economies have inexorably given rise to monopolistic-oligopolistic structures. Individuals do not bring equal skills and abilities to their economic activity. Those with greater skills earn more and can accumulate wealth in the form of private property. This concentrates economic power, a problem that is exacerbated by the granting of private property and accumulation rights to corporations. Eventually, the production and distribution activities are controlled by this accumulated economic power, which in turn limits the exercise of individual choice. The most serious aspect of this problem is the tendency for accumulation to end in unrestrained corporate growth. This causes the emergence of monopoly, oligopoly, and bureaucratic decision making. It feeds vested interest and allows producers to serve their own ends while ignoring societal welfare.

It is equally unacceptable to allow purely public decision making to be in control. Command economies have limited private choice and glorified public choice. The planning bureaucracy sets the goals and makes the implementation decisions. Both may be at variance with the needs of people.

Individual choice is tightly restricted and no direct mechanisms exist to allow people to influence or correct the decision-making process.

In both public and private decision-making models, bureaucratization limits options. Decisions are responsive to the interests of the organization rather than to human need. Some mix of private and public involvement seems inevitable. Even a purely private system that finds some way to avoid the problems of accumulation of power and growth of bureaucratic decision processes will not allow for the best possible range of alternatives. Kenneth Arrow has demonstrated that private choice models are not effective at providing social goods.[10] National defense, judicial systems, and highways are goods and services that cannot be produced and distributed through a private market economy. There must be some public-sector decision making in order to ensure production of adequate amounts of these public goods. A decision to build more roads, given limited resources, implies that less of something else will be produced. How should the different decision-making mechanisms interact to assure that the final mix of private and public goods maximizes the potential for choice?

Economic models do not answer these questions. To seek answers from analytic models argues for change that is an extension of the present. Change that is truly responsive to human need drives the system toward "what ought to be." No particular set of institutions guarantees an opening up of the future, an expansion of economic choice, and an enhancement of freedom. What is needed is not *the* system, but rather *a* system that develops the options in the light of human freedom, not vested interest.

The second pivotal economic issue requires that the maximization of choice take place without exploitative arrangements in the production process. When accumulated wealth is attuned to the service of self-interest, and when bureaucracies seek first their own survival, those without wealth and bureaucratic power will suffer. The normal economic model of exploitation shows some contributor to the production process (usually labor) receiving a reward less than its productive contribution.[11] This *can* happen: for example, a monopoly purchaser of labor may be able to force labor to work for too low a wage because there are no options for alternative employment. Such conditions have often led labor to organize in an effort to counteract the power of management. This exploitation is a problem, but not a very widespread one. The large corporations and other productive organizations that have the power to exploit are also in the position of selling their goods in monopoly or oligopoly markets. They can pass on wage increases in the form of higher prices. Therefore, maintenance of wages below productivity is not necessary. Labor peace is usually more profitable than low wages.[12] Exploitation of the consumer replaces exploitation of labor.

At another level, monopolies restrict output in order to raise profit and the oligopolies in the planning sector increase output in order to expand sales and revenue. In either case, society's resources, including labor, are wasted. Samuelson argues that the monopoly case represents " 'exploitation' of labor (and other transferable resources) in the sense that society's labor is misapplied as between goods and leisure or as between too-scarce monopolized goods in relation to too plentiful competitive goods."[13] It is possible that some workers will not be employed at all if monopoly power restricts output. Alternatively, necessary service functions may be slighted when the expansion of oligopoly firms draws labor away from the more competitive service sector, which cannot afford the higher wages. In either case, the monopoly power, however used, leads to an exploitive maldistribution of labor and to higher prices for consumers.

The large scale associated with industrial organizations leads to a third form of exploitation: a dehumanization of the work place. The widespread existence of huge, automated production facilities condemns workers to a monotonous and nonchallenging environment. This is symbolized most effectively by the General Motors Lordstown plant. Touted as the most modern auto production facility in the world, it has faced enormous productivity problems due to worker apathy and disaffection with its large size and the total impersonality that it has forced upon the workers. When assembly-line workers envision themselves only as interchangeable parts in a large machine, the production process begins to lose any human qualities. Depersonalization and dehumanization are endemic to the industrial world. Bureaucracies are concerned with growth and survival. Too much concern with individuals may lead to decisions that run counter to the continued existence of the bureaucracy. General Motors cannot be concerned with the welfare of each individual worker—that gets in the way of "efficiency." Highly regimented and depersonalized work environments maintain the critical distance that ensures the continued objectification of workers. If this were the only issue to be considered, it would be tempting to answer in the vein of E. F. Schumacher's *Small Is Beautiful,* and scale down all economic activity until depersonalization was no longer practical.[14] But large-scale production activity provides expanded material benefits, and that expands choice. The fact that accumulation and bureaucracy have led to dehumanized work environments should not serve as an excuse for sacrificing the choice aspects of human freedom. Desirable working environments are possible; they are not "convenient" when bureaucratic self-interest is placed ahead of human need.

Once large production bureaucracies are in place and have fully exploited the resources and markets of their domestic countries, external economic expansion is necessary for growth to continue. This constitutes a fourth form of exploitation. Nineteenth-century colonialism and twentieth-century imperialism are the most visible manifestations of this phenomenon. Its modern form in the capitalist countries is the multinational corporation, which is becoming the dominant economic force in the noncommunist world. Using Third World natural resources and labor supplies as a replacement for rapidly depleting domestic re-

sources and as a way to avoid unionization and higher
wages has been an important capitalist activity for many
years. Now the large corporations are using the Third
World as a marketplace. Corporate growth is being fueled
by the sale of goods to Third World countries. Those countries are having the structure of their choices defined by the
sales and resource needs of the multinational corporations.[15]

Dehumanization of labor in the industrialized world,
coupled with exploitation of the human and physical resources of the Third World, are the most obvious effects of
the struggle for survival and growth by bureaucratic production organizations. In capitalist societies the priority of
the profit motive ensures a masking of corporate actions
behind the screen of the neoclassical story with its invisible
hand and its assumptions of societal welfare. In addition,
various external threats such as the cold war or the oil crisis
serve to justify expansion and economic imperialism in the
name of important national priorities.

In modern industrial societies it is too often true that
people serve institutions rather than the reverse. In the
United States the institution of private property has been
elevated to a point where property rights clearly exceed
human rights. The right of a large corporation to build
facilities and use resources as it wishes is clearly dominant
over the right of the individual to have sufficient food, a
healthy environment, and decent working conditions. Too
often, the response to the starving is to give them a loaf of
bread. That may be a marvelous act of personal expiation,
but it does not address the fact that a system has been
created that permits starvation amidst plenty. The system
of private property rights which allows the owner to use
resources in virtually any way, no matter how wasteful or
extravagant, intercepts the need to build a new system in
which the starving can earn their loaf of bread.

If a new economic order is to arise, property rights will
have to be subordinated to human rights. All persons must
be allowed to contribute to and share the benefits of pro-

duction. There is a need for a management hierarchy, but the decision-making process should be shared with the labor force. The exercise of monopoly power should be turned toward societal need without the loss of benefits of large-scale production. The decision-making structure must be broadened so that there is no longer a gap between the decision makers and those affected by the decisions. The system must be torn away from concentration upon its own survival and forced into a widespread concern for human need. Such a change is revolutionary and can occur only via adoption of human goals for the production process. The vested interests that dominate current industrial systems must be eliminated so that institutions can serve people.

The last economic question to be addressed is that of distribution. How shall the fruits of the production process be distributed? Currently, distribution of income in industrial societies is closely aligned with the distribution of power. As Arrow points out, "the price system does not in any way prescribe a just distribution of income."[16] The powerful, either through ownership or through bureaucratic status, get the bulk of the income and the nonincome perquisites. This holds for command economies as well as market ones. In the Soviet Union a vacation home, preferential treatment in stores and restaurants, and the use of a car are all income emoluments awarded to high-ranking party members, government officials, and managers. In the United States, there may be more emphasis on money income, but the effect is the same. The usual justification for this in the market system is that productivity differences make for income differences.

The source of these real income differentials is rooted only loosely in productivity. The power of bureaucratic structures to insulate themselves from market forces means that the management of the bureaucracy can command extensive economic rewards largely unrelated to economic contribution. While the president of a major American corporation may have a significant impact on the success of that corporation, it is difficult to imagine a contribution as large as $500,000 or $750,000. Some portion of such salaries must be viewed as economic rent, an unearned increment created by the monopoly power of the corporation. Large profits are shared with top-level management. The second major source of income differentials is the accumulation of wealth, which becomes a source of larger future income. In the United States, the bulk of such wealth is either corporate or inherited and represents intergenerational accumulation. Thus, the income distribution is skewed toward those who already possess income and wealth and away from those who are propertyless. Even without inheritance, this phenomenon persists because those with more wealth and income in one generation have the ability to give their children greater educational opportunity and hence an income earning advantage over those whose parents do not possess such wealth and income.

The income differentials are not just reflected in the high incomes of a small segment of the society, however. They are tragically present in the poverty and dehumanizing physical conditions of many, particularly those facing discrimination because of race, sex, or age. The current distribution of income does not take enough account of the human need represented by these poverty conditions. But the conditions are just symptoms; the disease lies in a system that responds so strongly to economic power and so weakly to the cry of human need. Humanizing the distribution of income would redress current injustices and ensure access to income based on human need.

The agenda established for economics calls for the provision of choice that responds to the needs of individuals; it requires systems of production that exploit neither labor nor the consumer; and, it demands mechanisms of distribution that fulfill human need rather than strengthening vested interests.

Any substantial restructuring of society must begin with the sources of economic power. That power arises primarily from accumulated wealth and bureaucracy. The first step in reordering the priorities should be a tax that would transfer control of accumulated wealth away from large corporations and financial institutions. The government would pass the tax receipts on to workers and other people so that the control and use of wealth would be at the service of individual and societal needs. This would begin the process of income redistribution and would also change the source of investment decision making, thus broadening the locus of choice in the productive sphere.

The drive to accumulate is so strong that redistribution of wealth will not long constrain the misuse of power that comes from accumulated wealth. There must also be severe limitations upon the property rights of corporations. New laws and structures can prevent them from using their accumulated profit and ownership of capital to enhance their economic power. These should include restrictions on the ability of large corporations to use accumulated assets for investment in new businesses or product lines. Integration and merger should not be allowed unless they pass the strictest possible test of serving human need. With limited options for corporate expansion, much profit would be channeled into financial institutions to earn interest income. Therefore, potential growth of those institutions would also need to be limited and directed toward societal welfare by strict regulation of lending activities.

Creation of more humane and nonexploitive work environments can begin with the creation of new structures that allow more worker and public involvement in business decisions. Ultimately, wealth and inheritance taxes as well as profit could be used in part to create worker ownership. The human need for a fulfilling work environment would not continue to be subjugated to the pursuit of profit and growth if workers became the owners and managers of the productive corporations.[17]

Accumulated wealth and bureaucratic power have created an income distribution that significantly hinders the fulfillment of human freedom for a large segment of the population. Establishing a wealth tax, limiting the power of productive and financial corporations, and creating worker ownership and management will affect some of the distributional problems. However, they will not remove the effects of past maldistribution. At the very least, the choices available to all people must include adequate amounts of food, clothing, and shelter, easy access to health care, and equality of educational opportunity. Redressing past maldistribution in these areas can begin by directing some of the proceeds of the tax on wealth into the creation of an institutional structure that would provide these choices for everyone in the society.

All of these proposals only represent a modest beginning to the process of institutional creation and dismantling that must proceed if the liberation agenda is to be pursued and a new economic order is to emerge. Even these ideas are profoundly challenging to the existing order. The prevailing story argues that only moderate and gradual change is acceptable. Anything that is too strident or too radical must be discarded. That story must be rejected if we are to create time and space for freedom and respond to the cry of human need. We must ignore those voices which call for gradualism but which envision no real change in the existing power structure.

While the prevailing story calls for gradualism, moderation, and restraint, the reality of American existence has not always been marked by these themes. It is true that gradual change has been the dominant pattern of social behavior in most of the industrialized world, but it is not true that all of this change has been accomplished by peaceful means and personal restraint. The increased social and economic status of the laborer in the United States has resulted from a long and bitter struggle between labor unions on the one side and management, ownership, and government on the other. The result has been a gradual concession to the claims of labor, but the process was profoundly revolutionary and certainly neither peaceful nor restrained. The conditions of the poor, the disadvantaged and the suffering today are no different than the conditions of the industrial laborers in the nineteenth and early twentieth centuries.

The process of freeing them from oppression should not be impeded by appeals to gradualism and restraint, which in reality doom them to a continued existence at the margins of society. The complete fulfillment of the liberation agenda will always remain an ideal. However, it is possible to begin shaping institutions and structures of the society toward the goals of human freedom. Reorienting the uses of accumulated wealth and redirecting the goals of bureaucratic structures can be accomplished by dismantling some of the structures of society and creating new ones attuned to human need and human freedom. There can be a world in which the Eli Blacks are not crushed between conflicting claims for their allegiance.

Notes

1. James P. Rakowski and J. C. Johnson, "Airline Deregulation: Problems and Prospects," *Quarterly Review of Economics and Business,* Winter 1979, pp. 65–78; L. McDonald, "The Energy Tax Act of 1978," *Natural Resources Journal,* October 1979, pp. 859–69.

2. John Kenneth Galbraith, *Economics and the Public Purpose* (Boston: Houghton Mifflin, 1973), pp. 81–175.

3. Louis M. Kohlmeier, Jr., *The Regulators* (New York: Harper and Row, 1969), pp. 69–82.

4. Galbraith, *Economics and the Public Purpose,* pp. 317–24.

5. James W. Kuhn, "To Whom and for What Are Business Managers Responsible?" paper presented to a seminar on corporate responsibility at Catholic University of America, June 1978.

6. Thorstein Veblen, *The Vested Interests and the Common Man* (New York: Viking Press, 1946), p. 34.

7. Galbraith, *Economics and the Public Purpose,* pp. 92–109.

8. Wassily Leontief and George McGovern, "On Taxing and Redistributing Income," in David Mermelstein, ed., *Economics: Mainstream Readings and Radical Critiques,* 2nd ed. (New York: Random House, 1973), pp. 262–70.

9. See Henry Pachter, "Freedom, Authority, Participation," *Dissent,* Summer 1978, pp. 294–309.

10. Kenneth J. Arrow, *The Limits of Organization* (New York: Norton, 1974), pp. 22–24.

11. Nancy Smith Barrett, *The Theory of Microeconomic Policy* (Lexington, Mass.: D. C. Heath, 1974), p. 250.

12. Galbraith, *Economics and the Public Purpose*, p. 118.

13. Paul A. Samuelson, *Economics*, 9th ed. (New York: McGraw-Hill, 1973), p. 502.

14. E. F. Schumacher, *Small Is Beautiful: Economics As If People Mattered* (New York: Harper and Row, 1976).

15. See, for example, Louis Turner, *Multinational Companies and the Third World* (New York: Hill and Wang, 1973); or Richard J. Barnet and Ronald E. Muller, *Global Reach* (New York: Simon and Schuster, 1974).

16. Arrow, *The Limits of Organization*, p. 22.

17. See, for example, Michael Walzer, "Town Meetings and Workers' Control," *Dissent,* Summer 1978, pp. 325–33.

9 Overcoming the Existing Order

There is an inevitable tension between being a white, middle-class, American male and being under the impact of liberation theology. One's instincts and one's wits are out of phase at every significant point. Our interiority is set for other directions than the agenda liberation demands. Those who seek to align themselves with a history of freedom have a history of their own fashioned by advantages and attitudes, long cherished and ingrained, that inhibit the freedom of others. Liberation theology calls for a steady process of reinventing ourselves against a self-creation durably in force. Our inner history runs in the wrong direction. Being "born again" may have a time and place for some, but for most of us the conversion from our role as oppressors to the actualization of freedom in our world and within ourselves occurs in our moments of decision each day. We daily experience ourselves as the battleground between an open future and futurelessness. The struggle between the private and the corporate self is a permanent feature of our existence. It is never resolved, but reappears in each new moment. It is tempting and even therapeutic to join with Martin Luther in throwing inkwells at the devil, but the demons originate within, and in the naming and renaming of ourselves their expulsion begins. It is a beginning without end. The consequence is that we bring an uncommon intensity to common polarities in our culture.

A. Contemplation and Action

One of the most obvious of polarities is the one between contemplation and action, being and doing, spirituality and

215

worldly intervention. The individual experiences the options of getting oneself together in relation to the Ultimate or altering society in order to make it conform more nearly to the intentions of the Ultimate. While the issue is an ancient one, a recent phenomenon is particularly interesting. Many of those who were compulsive activists in the 1960s became chronic exponents of meditation and interiority in the 1970s. The flip between the modalities is decisive but leaves one wondering about the formation of the problem. Must one opt for either contemplation or the arena of action?

A way of backing into the issue is to expose the degree to which each can be a flight from the other. Often those who have taken to the streets play out unresolved internal problems through their protests and acts of intervention. At best they hope that their identity will come together along the way. In contrast, often those who immerse themselves in forms of contemplation flee from responsibility for their worldly setting. Their ability to cope in the larger arena is undisciplined for want of daily risk in relation to their environment. Jürgen Moltmann states the peril clearly: "Anyone who falls back on activity because he cannot come to terms with himself . . . is merely a burden to other people. Activity and political commitment for the liberation of the oppressed are not a panacea against feebleness of the personality and lazy thinking. It is only the person who finds himself who can give himself. It is only the one who has become free that can free others."[1] Our social environment and the religious scene present us with the option of piety or justice. In the measure we succumb to that dichotomy we risk enslaving others in our crusades for freedom or leaving others in their slavery while we "manicure our souls."

A rebirth in our relationship to hope should not emerge through the story of Sara and Abraham without consideration of the story of the transfiguration as interpreted in chapter 1. Most would agree that the exercises which restore wholeness and those which call for change under

the imperatives of the future belong together. Futurelessness within and futurelessness without are obvious correlates. When the future begins to hold sway in the person but
not in the societal order—or the reverse—the process is
perverse and the consequences often pernicious. Internal
authority and external freedom are intrinsic to each other's
fulfillment.

For liberation theology, contemplation and action are
both worldly forms of existence. Times for piety and times
for politics share a focus upon the very "materiality" of
God's being in the world. The earlier discussion of God's
glory and God's justice stands guard over a disposition to
enjoy God out of this world and serve the deity in it. One of
the peculiarities in the encounter with the biblical God is
that we are continually given the world again. The radicality of the "word made flesh" forbids the dichotomizing
many of us recognize in ourselves. Being grasped by God
and by the world then become two aspects of one apprehension. Henri Nouwen argues for an understanding of their
interpenetration: "Christian life is not a life divided between times for action and times for contemplation. No.
Real social action is a way of contemplation, and real contemplation is the core of social action. In the final analysis,
action and contemplation are two sides of the same reality
which makes man an agent of change."[2]

The collusion of contemplation and action may be seen in
the act of prayer. There is something ironic and forceful
about making the case on this particular form of traditional
piety. In our culture prayer has become increasingly prob-
lematic. Where it is in force, it often appears to be a flight
from worldly engagement. For those of us brought up in
churches that did pray for the hungry and naked, the liturgies seemed empty and even obscene when we intended to
do nothing costly ourselves. Prayer can become the
medium through which we do nothing but pay our respects
to an aspect of biblical tradition. That is obviously a prostitution of the manner in which Jesus taught his disciples to
pray. "When the disciples approached Jesus, asking him to

teach them to pray, he taught them words whose real meaning they discovered only later. . . . . The only way those words could become prayer would be if they were offered in the context of their world and the environment around them. . . . prayer means relating words to reality."[3] And that, for most of us, demands relearning and retooling ourselves.

The transformation of prayer begins in our focus upon the one to whom we pray. The dialogue partner makes the crucial difference. The "god" of American civil religion makes no claims upon us that call for radical revisions in our relation to our environment. Indeed, that "god" enables us to live at peace with the order of our world and points us to personal piety as our controlling need. But the God who is present in the other and calls for solidarity, who participates in our suffering, whom to know is to do justice, and whose ineffableness is a prelude to our relinquishment— that dialogue partner initiates the relearning process. Words thought to be the same are radically different when part of our prayer life. The hungry and naked are no longer statistics and abstractions. They are the presence of God in the present formation of pain and suffering. God's participation in our materiality transforms the words we use and their impact upon us. In the process of putting our situation into words we are now acknowledging God's own involvement. That raises the stakes immeasurably! We recognize and handle the world differently when the God affirmed in liberation theology is our partner.

Prayer now becomes subversive, the means by which we begin to free ourselves of contentment and concurrence with the present as it is given to us. It is one of the means of passage from the story of accommodation to the story of death and resurrection in the Gospel. Prayer is a deprogramming, a process of liberation from our age. As an act of discernment it is the beginning of engagement with the world in terms of what is intended by the God of freedom. Prayer leads to watchfulness and sensitivity for justice. "No one who prays in Christ's name and cries out for redemption can put up with oppression. No one who fights against injustice can dispense with prayer for redemption. The more Christians intervene for the life of the hungry, the human rights of the oppressed and the fellowship of the forsaken, the deeper they will be led into continual prayer."[4] Contemplation and action have a fusion in the unity of faith and love. They open into each other and demand each other with an overlapping apprehension of the world and God. Reading the Bible and reading the newspaper become at some point one event, even as prayer and restructuring the economic order converge and become inseparable.

B. Submission and Subversion

A second polarity is that between submission to the authorities under whose jursidiction we fall and subversion of their exercise of power.

In its most extreme form, submission is expressed in the slogan, "America, love it or leave it." The only alternative to willing consent is departure. Those who choose to wrap the issue in biblical authority may appeal to the thirteenth chapter of Romans. A surface reading is clear and explicit enough: "Let every person be subject to the governing authorities. For there is no authority except from God, and those that exist have been instituted by God" (Romans 13:1). Resistance is finally rebellion against God. One need not be a redneck to find an element of the argument appealing. Instinctively we appeal to the notion that order is preferable to chaos. Life is more likely to be tolerable and productive if we come under some form of jurisdiction. One need not go all the way to "law and order" to appreciate the freedom that may be occasioned by a significant component of order.

Our personal disposition toward order is legitimated on the larger scale by American civil religion. At one level it can be understood as an attempt to provide community or a sense of peoplehood. With its provision of a sense of why we are here, whence we came, and our destiny under God, the present order is affirmed. Obviously, it is not the case that there is an explicit confirmation. Civil religion at its worst may legitimate the perverse but at its best it implicitly legitimates the arrangements of our common life. One has only to resist those arrangements to realize the degree to which participation in community is a function of consent to the structures, rituals, and symbols that support it. Those who evoke a remembered history at odds with the established ways are placed in peril. The system takes care of itself.

Whether one follows one's instincts or the ethos provided by civil religion, the thrust of our common life is toward submission as the means of preserving the journey toward freedom. Indeed, boundaries and authorities enable the processes of freedom to occur.

But subversion is a possibility as well, and for some the only one. The premise ruling this posture is that the systems of order inevitably fall under evil and perpetuate the denial of freedom. It is not merely that power corrupts but that power itself is corrupt. Its organizing of the chaos is inherently pernicious. This world is ruled by "principalities and powers" destined to prevent our common life and personal quests.

We need not rehearse the themes of institutions outliving their usefulness, of the persistence of the neoclassical story, or of the bureaucratic decision-making processes that dominate industrial societies. These themes define the boundaries and authorities under which we live. If these structures do not serve the interests of human freedom, then why do we countenance their continued existence? If immersion in the present does indeed constitute the leitmotif of these institutions and structures, then how can we hope to use such structures to eliminate futurelessness?

The book of Revelation, and chapter 13 in particular, can be invoked as biblical warrant for subversion as the only posture. The issue, then, is not wicked men in high places but the corruption of all those places. To be true to life is to be in perpetual rebellion against all forms of authority. In the book of Revelation the destruction of Babylon is parabolic; it expresses the manner and degree to which the provision of order in society is permeated by demonic forces. The triumph of the demonic is not primarily in the sphere of individual consciousness but in the orders of society. Because they are "governed by the power of death," their "dehumanizing influence" is pervasive and sure.[5] The great truth about our common life is that it is possessed by demons with total jurisdiction over the very orders that presume to provide freedom. The book of Revelation thus has as an underlying theme the contention that our world is fallen and in every way is organized to "assault, captivate, enslave, and dominate human beings" in ways that erase their moral and rational capacity for freedom.[6] In response, one can only assume a posture of resistance to every form of oppression with which we are confronted.

While it may be the case that our instincts are set for submission, most of us have no corresponding aptitude for subversion—all the more so in those of us for whom, on the surface at least, the prevailing arrangements provide our advantages. It would appear initially as if we had only the options of being dupes or compulsive revolutionaries. Much that is written in the realm of liberation theology is an attempt to promote our passage from the model sanctioned by American civil religion to that of revolt. One is left with the feeling that the only way to be faithful to God is to be faithless to one's homeland. If that be the case, the enlistments will be few indeed and the futility more strident. Numbers, of course, are not the measure of justice and the rightness of a cause, but any apparent license for freedom against one's society carries with it a capacity for evil that denies freedom in its name.

It is important to affirm that nothing in the biblical material authorizes subversion as a moral norm. What we have are "liberative memories."[7] The Exodus event is a stunning example of defiance of Egyptian rule by the Israelites, but it does not function as an obligation for all persons at all times. It does function as a form of permission; subversion is a possibility. Remembering the Exodus nourishes "Christian consciousness, give[s] inspiration to the imagination of faith, and prompt[s] people to liberative action."[8] Through its agency, the fear of revolution is dispelled and we are allowed to entertain the possibility of insurrection as a course that may be compatible with faith. The Exodus lives in memory, then, as a way of allowing action from which we instinctively recoil as illicit. It frees us from a perverted notion of patriotism and all the subtle restraints it imposes.

It is equally important to affirm that the biblical material does not make submission a moral norm or obligation. It may be that the most advantageous place to make that case is within the text used most frequently to warrant submission. Obviously there is nothing in Romans 13 that legitimates a just rebellion, but we misunderstand it if we read it as advocating unjust submission. At a minimum we need to recognize that the author is specifically addressing the situation of Roman Christians in the first century—not every political reality. To ignore the particularity and construct a platitude readily applicable whenever needed is an exercise in nonhistorical exegesis. The only supportable line of argument is that submission or nonresistance may be a legitimate course of action for the faithful—as indeed it was for Roman Christians in the first century.

Beyond the historical context, we must be attentive to the literary one. Chapters 12 and 13 in the book of Romans form a unit. To read the latter as if the former did not exist is a violation of the text. Chapter 12 clearly authorizes nonconformity as a legitimate posture. The nature of God's merciful activity is invoked as the basis upon which one need not accept the present arrangements as binding. The action of God precipitates changes and is an invitation to partnership. "Any interpretation of 13:1–7 that would make it the expression of a static or conservative undergirding of the present social system would therefore represent a refusal to take seriously the context."[9] And, of course, reading in chapter 13 beyond 1–7 introduces dimensions that would intercept sanctioning and submission. What we have in chapter 13, then, is a recognition of "giveness" rather than legitimacy. What is given will be used by God, but not endorsed.

At one level, Romans 13 invokes caution as appropriate to the Christian community at that time and place. The orders of the old age remain in force; the new era exists as promise. The author is intercepting a fanatical disposition to freedom that would take form among the early Christians if they thought that the new day had already been inaugurated. Perhaps the pivotal and controlling line in the chapter is verse 10: "Love does no wrong to a neighbor: therefore love is the fulfilling of the law." The Christian community is to attend to that obligation and let their "submission to the state . . . [take] the form of negative obedience amounting to indifference."[10] What is binding upon me is "neighbor love." But neither submission nor legitimation is the thrust of the chapter. What is legitimated, and cause for submission, is the faith claim that God will make all things new in the power of love.

Christianity has been used as an agency of restraint since the time of Constantine. It has nourished the disposition to order and harmony. Exploiters of the tradition have invoked it to diminish the tension between the "is" and the "ought to be" in our world. That, alas, is the ultimate perversion of Christianity's message. An authentic reading of the Gospel allows for times of submission, which are acts of indifference rather than legitimation, but just as readily it permits subversion or insurrection as a form of faithfulness to love. Its "liberative memories" set precedents that may become obligations for us without being moral norms.

The perversion of the Christian message is a cogent example of the need to maintain a subversive posture. If a message and an institution whose avowed goals have been the freeing and humanizing of people can be made to serve less lofty ends, how much more may other institutions that possess no such high ideal be twisted? Indeed, since the

American economic system grows out of ideals of self-interest espoused in the neoclassical story, why should we ever assume that the system would continue to serve the best interests of the society at large?

C. Reformation and Revolution

A third polarity is that between reformation and revolution. While in some ways an extension of the previous polarity, it nevertheless is an advance in the formulation of the means by which we are faithful to the future.

Once again, many of our instincts lead to the posture that affirms incremental change as the most viable and durable. The reform of our systems, their modification and alteration, is the maneuver that will facilitate the journey toward freedom for all. Underneath the argument is a sense that systems are fundamentally benign. While they may embody the evil disposition of human beings, there is no intrinsic relationship between the systems and the forces of oppression. With new persons and new values, the needs of all can be met. One remembers the moment when Chief Justice Warren Burger had sworn in Gerald Ford as president following the resignation of Richard Nixon and was heard to say with a sigh of relief, "The system works." Alas, it did. Perhaps to Americans the chief justice expressed the cornerstore of their credo: our systems may need to be revised, inflated, restored, but fundamentally they are sound and work to our advantage.

While that confidence is imbedded in and nourished by American civil religion, some would call up biblical evidence for it as well. As we have argued earlier, one can present a case that depicts Jesus as being rather indifferent to systemic change. Particularly outside the religious realm, the evidence is scant that he targeted the systems of his day for destruction. And one would be hard pressed to dispute the support in the biblical records for change that is orderly and within the bounds of tradition at its best. With respect to the law in its most obvious form, Jesus' Sermon on the Mount is a significant paradigm. While the rhetoric follows the line, "you have heard it said of old, but I say to you," the substance of the charge is substantial yet not so radical as to remove the linchpin from the Jewish heritage.

Most of us are less ready to invest credibility in the option of revolution. The reasons are many and rather obvious. Some have to do with motives and consequences. In the early 1970s Peter Berger and Richard J. Neuhaus published an analysis of American radicalism in the form of a debate over the conservative versus the revolutionary. What was particularly revealing was that Berger laid out a series of maxims addressed to the radical which Neuhaus never contested. Underneath each maxim was a presumption of guilt—guilty until proved innocent with respect to motives and rationality. "Only believe those whose motives are compassionate and whose programs stand the test of rational inquiry. . . . When it comes to the revolutionaries, only trust the sad ones. The enthusiastic ones are the oppressors of tomorrow—or else they are kidding. . . . Listen to their voices. Watch for the signals of compassion. Watch how they laugh."[11] There is considerable wisdom in those maxims and their value in sorting out our personal complicity in our actions is evidence enough. But no similar maxims were developed for the conservatives. The burden of proof only fell upon one side of the argument. This is but one manifestation of our disposition to trust those who argue for gradualism and distrust those advocating a radical posture.

The term *revolution* covers so many possibilities that its use invokes a range of responses and aversions. It tends for many to be synonymous with overthrowing the government and acts of violence. In the context of our polarity, revolution means two things. The first is that the systems themselves are not benign but in fact bear an intrinsic relationship to values that may prevent the openness of the future. Reform presupposes systemic innocence and looks for improvisations that will repair the system's flaws. Second, the entrenchment and perniciousness of systems may require degrees and kinds of action that in principle one would not prefer or perhaps condone. Certain actions to intercept the impact of a system on individuals may be necessary but not justifiable. When James Cone and others talk of freedom by "whatever means necessary," there is more at stake than not bargaining away your trump card. Creating "time and space for freedom" may necessitate actions difficult to defend in the abstract. One thinks of Dietrich Bonhoeffer, the pacifist, finally participating in the plot to assassinate Hitler—doing it, but not defining it as a model of Christian response. To envision a world in which reformation and moderation are the only paths necessary to overcome futurelessness is to create an illusion. The structural basis of industrial societies is so firmly set and immersion in the present so pervasive that it is difficult to imagine a world in which the journey toward freedom is aligned for very long with goals of existing authority. We need to recognize the prevalence of violence both in the changes that are accomplished and in the ways the structures attempt to prevent change. Once this is recognized, the legitimation of only certain kinds of revolution crumbles.

The difference, then, between reformation and revolution lies in our perception of the permanence of existing systems and our determination to transcend them by whatever means are necessary. The feature of Christian history that is sometimes most evident is a disposition to blunt the cry of pain and restrain the force of humane responses. While it is not the only or even the controlling theme in the black religious tradition, it is not difficult to lift out those components that were used to encourage slaves to make peace with their circumstances. It is this point of vulnerability that leads a Third World theologian to say, "Perhaps the first important contribution Christians can make to the process of liberation is not to add to the process of diluting the revolutionary implications that circumstances have dictated it should contain."[12] The issue then becomes one of identifying what in the Christian tradition offsets the tendency to sanction systems and comfort the afflicted within their circumstances.

The reality of Jesus is the centerpiece in any answer to the question. An earlier argument showed that there is no warrant for constructing a picture of Jesus as a party-line revolutionary. He was not a Zealot. Yet, in a more subtle sense, what is known about Jesus certainly points to "the introduction into history of a subversive power which negates the old to make room for the new."[13] The Gospel of Jesus and the phenomenon of revolution overlap in a sturdy commitment to transformation of the present in the light of the anticipated future. There is a clear distinction between the old and the new along with the consequences that follow as the one breaks in upon the other. The transfiguration story is the earnest of that. For us "to attain the image of Christ means to live in revolt against the great pharaoh and to remain with the oppressed and the disadvantaged."[14] The element of the transfiguration story that banks toward revolution needs careful exposition.

Karl Barth develops the theme of Jesus as the agency of God's permanent revolution and the basis for distrust of the existing orders on theological grounds. God is "the one who breaks all bonds asunder, in new historical developments and situations each of which is for those who can see and hear—only a sign, but an unmistakable sign, of His freedom and kingdom and over-ruling of history."[15] The effect of the event is to make clear that all the orders of life have legitimate claim to no more than "transitory validity." They are not "vitally necessary and absolutely authoritative even for their own time and sphere." Yet, having said that, Barth claims there is a "passive conservatism of Jesus" at significant points. Many things that one might have expected him to bring under attack, he let be. Jesus did not challenge the temple as his Father's house; he respected the order of the family, he adapted to practices of the synagogue; he appears to have avoided direct conflict with the economic order of the day, and he recognized political authority even in the case of Pilate in relation to himself. He revealed "provisional and qualified respect" in the presence of the existing orders.[16]

While Jesus existed within the framework of existing orders, he consistently made it evident they were not binding on him or his followers. While not challenging the existence of the temple, he made it clear that there was something greater than it; while affirming the honor of the family, he could transpose his family allegiance in decisive ways; while accepting the prevailing practices of religion, he could preempt them at particular moments; while taking for granted much of the economic and political orders, he could participate in striking breaches of their authority.[17] But these particular instances are not the primary thrust of the crisis in the human order created by Jesus. The most telling point in his message is the incompatibility of the old and new as evident in Mark 2:21. The discussion of new cloth and old garment, old wineskins and new wines, boldly states "the radical and indissolvable antithesis of the kingdom of God to all human kingdoms."[18] In the message of Jesus, the existing orders are the old garments and old bottles that must give way under the new. A true conservatism presupposes a compatibility of the old and the new, while Jesus is maintaining that the one is finally destructive of the other. The Gospel message cannot abide the premises upon which reform rests or allow for a dilution of the tension between the kingdom of God and all human orders. For Barth, revolution comes from God and not from the revolt of persons who are afflicted.

Jesus, as God's permanent revolution, is the point of radical delegitimizing of existing orders. He stands for a future at odds with any conditions that prevail and demands their breach or even their destruction. In the interim, reformation may be an option, but finally nothing can stand against the revolution whose origin is in God's action for freedom. Both American civil religion and the prevailing economic order are doomed.

D. Liberation and Reconciliation

A final polarity is between liberation and reconciliation, between what is required to make time and space for freedom and the act of forgiveness through which reunion of the separated occurs. Any reordering of present structures is not likely to occur as a result of gradual evolution or from a magnanimous gesture on the part of vested interests. The agenda for the future will inevitably cause ruptures within and between persons as well as in their relationships to the social order. The journey toward freedom seldom occurs without substantial fallout. Privilege and power do not normally yield with a sigh of relief. Most individuals are not waiting for the opportunity to engage in relinquishment, and even if they were, the structures of the social order are set to sustain oppression. One ought not understate the symbolic impact of a body of persons who might want to divest themselves of material advantage and lead a more lean existence on behalf of the deprived, but the economic and political realities built into our systems and institutions will keep the poor in poverty. Only action that incapacitates those phenomena and replaces them with others that serve humane values can make a significant difference. Liberation from the oppression imbedded in the orders of society is unavoidably disruptive at one level or another and finally sets father against son, mother against daughter. We ought not retreat from the realization that those who make the journey toward freedom are troublemakers in human and institutional terms.

The bibilical theme of reconciliation involves a union of the separated. It calls for a quality of forgiveness that enables the dividing wall of hostility to crumble under the impact of grace. Most of our images, clustered around themes like "the brotherhood of man under the fatherhood of God," summon up the aspiration for harmony and mutual bonding. Singing "black and white together" means for many a mutuality uncontaminated by the realities of oppression in our history. Reconciliation comes to imply that nothing that has gone before exists in the present. Whites expect blacks to throw the past into the past and embrace them as agents of goodwill. Whatever strident claims blacks make for compensatory action or for separatism in various forms are read as covering all past sins, thus "making all things new." There is a level at which the oppressed will not be reconciled, for it would mean a confirmation of their loss of freedom and a dilution of their dignity. Any vision of reconciliation that summons forth a coming together as if the barriers did not continue to exist is a denial of freedom.

We readily understand that liberation has a political as well as a private thrust, but forgiveness has been privatized to the point where it is equated with interpersonal harmony. Thus it is easy to understand why the agenda becomes one of reunion without any alteration in the balance of power and privilege. Obviously, a privatized version of sin is a prelude to that position. But sin is also a political event. It is imbedded in structures and nourished through their perpetuation. It is difficult for the oppressed to relate to forgiveness; it is mediated where they least need it—that is, at the points of their personal stress—not where they have a primary need for a new beginning. It is not an internal journey toward freedom that is denied but one in the social order. Grace for the oppressed is when institutions and systems that have sapped their possibilities and rights are lifted from their backs. Grace is whatever systemic revision brings food to the hungry, clothing to the naked, visitation to those in prison, and vision to the blind—not as acts of charity but as rights to be seized. In the late sixties many blacks called for reparations. Most whites responded from the sense that they owed nothing for whatever advantages their forefathers had reaped from blacks. What they failed to grasp was that the message of forgiveness could only occur in a redressing of the imbalance of power. In our society, wealth is power—the power to enable the conditions of freedom to occur. Forgiveness is first an act of reparation that restores human agency and power to an oppressed people, and secondarily an experience of mutuality between persons and races. Forgiveness means changing the conditions of the past before calling for a reunion of the separated.

Some of the tension between liberation and reconciliation is reduced when we recognize the political character of both. But the deeper meaning in their relationship lies in the realization of the cost factor in both. There is neither liberation nor reconciliation without an element of suffering participation in the process. Authentic forgiveness occurs only where the offender moves toward the offended through the full measure of the anguish and alienation that the oppression has caused. Any initiatives that bypass the wounds have no capacity to heal. Only anguish can touch anguish and redress the broken network of relationships. Liberation has its price as well. The oppressors must hurt, they must participate in the situations they have created by their inhumanity. Charity cannot create a liberating environment. There is no substitute for the oppressors living in the fullness of the reality they have created. That is a prelude to the costly forms of relinquishment required of us. The situation of freedom is double-edged. There is a loss of humanity in those who deny dignity and rights as well as in the victims. A process of "conscientization" must occur in the life of both the oppressed and the oppressor. Then the liberation can begin and reconciliation is a possibility.

Thus, at a distant point reconciliation and liberation merge into one. But as we enter the condition of oppression, liberation has priority. Reconciliation can be used as a weapon to impede the agenda of freedom and enable us to be timid in the face of monstrous evil. It is a great irony that grace can be used to break the journey toward freedom by those who sanctify their own benefits with religious rhetoric. Albert Camus seems to have captured the force of that when he wrote, "only two possible worlds can exist for the human mind: the sacred world and the world of rebellion."[19] Camus's point is that grace and revolt are antithetical phenomena. Rebellion is life affirming as a passionate exercise in protest against inhumanity, while grace comes into play as tolerance for the conditions that obtain. On the deeper level that need not be so. Yet Camus is describing what, in fact, occurs when reconciliation is the controlling theme that sets boundaries for liberation.

Through these chapters many of us may have begun to identify ourselves as those whose personal histories and social structures have secured futurelessness and impeded the journey of others toward freedom. We are not black or female or Third World citizens. Our linkage is with those who have access to the levers that hold others down. However, the analysis of economic policy has disclosed our powerlessness before the very structures we sanction—at least by our silence. The naming of our complicity should lead beyond mere guilt—which brings personal expiation but results only in erratic and ineffectual action at the societal level. The human vocation is finally to resist the forms of futurelessness that engulf us all and to provide our commonality as sisters and brothers.

Because our lineage is with the oppressors, we continue to be the victims of our own advantages. Our instincts lead us toward contemplation rather than action, submission rather than subversion, and reform rather than revolution. For the best of reasons and with the worst of consequences we invoke the theme of reconciliation as the price of liberation becomes clearer. We choose welfare handouts to treat symptoms rather than systemic revolution to treat causes. But when we really listen to the pain our world inflicts and the promise the biblical message erects, we reach for the grounds of hope and courage. They are not within ourselves. Nor are they within any present arrangements or their modifications. The enactment of a new future is a possibility because the journey toward freedom in our world is the awesome pilgrimage of God. Through that alone can we resist the temptation to settle for the "cold logic of human reason," or to erect "three booths" through which to sanction a present whose future is in the past. Accommodation is no longer acceptable. The "wild, irrational hope" engendered by "the God of hope" makes the possibility of the impossible an obligation and the human privilege.

Notes

1. Jürgen Moltmann, *The Church in the Power of the Spirit* (New York: Harper and Row, 1977), pp. 285–86.

2. Henri Nouwen, *Creative Ministry* (Garden City, N.Y.: Doubleday, 1971), p. 87.

3. Michael H. Crosby, *Thy Will Be Done* (Maryknoll, N.Y.: Orbis Books, 1977), p. 7.

4. Moltmann, *The Church in the Power of the Spirit*, p. 287.

5. William Stringfellow, *An Ethic for Christians and Other Aliens in a Strange Land* (Waco, Tex.: Word Press, 1973), p. 32.

6. Ibid., p. 97.

7. Alfredo Fierro, *The Militant Gospel* (Maryknoll, N.Y.: Orbis Books, 1977), p. 129–81.

8. Ibid., p. 149.

9. John Howard Yoder, *The Politics of Jesus* (Grand Rapids, Mich.: Eerdmans, 1972), p. 198.

10. Paul Lehmann, *The Transfiguration of Politics* (New York: Harper and Row, 1975), p. 38.

11. Peter Berger and Richard J. Neuhaus, *Movement and Revolution* (Garden City, N.Y.: Doubleday, 1970), p. 19.

12. Hugo Assmann, *Theology for a Nomad Church* (Maryknoll, N.Y.: Orbis Books, 1976), p. 129.

13. J. G. Davies, *Christian, Politics and Violent Revolution* (Maryknoll, N.Y.: Orbis Books, 1976), p. 100.

14. Dorothee Söelle, *Suffering* (Philadelphia: Fortress Press, 1975), p. 132.

15. Karl Barth, *Church Dogmatics*, vol. 4, part 2 (Edinburgh: T. & T. Clark, 1958), p. 173.

16. Ibid., pp. 173–75.

17. Ibid., pp. 175–76.

18. Ibid., p. 177.

19. Albert Camus, *The Rebel: An Essay on Man in Revolt*, trans. Anthony Bower (New York: Vintage Books, 1956), p. 21.

Bibliography

Adams, Walter, ed. *The Structure of American Industry*. 5th ed. New York: Macmillan, 1977.

Alves, Rubem. *A Theology of Human Hope*. Washington/Cleveland: Corpus Books, 1969.

Arrow, Kenneth J. "A Cautious Case for Socialism." *Dissent*, Fall 1978.

──────. *The Limits of Organization*. New York: W. W. Norton, 1974.

Assmann, Hugo. *Theology for a Nomad Church*. Maryknoll, N.Y.: Orbis Books, 1976.

Barbour, Ian G. *Myths, Models, and Paradigms*. New York: Harper and Row, 1974.

Barnet, Richard J., and Muller, Ronald E. *Global Reach*. New York: Simon and Schuster, 1974.

Barrett, Nancy Smith. *The Theory of Microeconomic Policy*. Lexington, Mass.: D. C. Heath, 1974.

Barth, Karl. *Church Dogmatics*. Vol. 3, part 4. Edinburgh: T. & T. Clark, 1961.

──────. *Church Dogmatics*. Vol. 4, part 2. Edinburgh: T. & T. Clark, 1958.

──────. *The Epistle to the Romans*. Fair Lawn, N.J.: Oxford University Press, 1953.

Bellah, Robert N. *The Broken Covenant*. New York: Seabury Press, 1975.

──────. "The Revolution and Civil Religion." In *Religion and the American Revolution*, Jerald C. Brauer et al. Philadelphia: Fortress Press, 1976.

Bennett, John, "Fitting the Liberation Theme into Our Theological Agenda." *Christianity and Crisis*, July 18, 1977.

Berger, Peter, and Neuhaus, Richard J. *Movement and Revolution.* Garden City, N.Y.: Doubleday, 1970.

Berger, Peter. *The Precarious Vision.* Garden City, N.Y.: Doubleday, 1961.

————. *A Rumor of Angels.* Garden City, N.Y.: Doubleday, 1969.

————. *The Sacred Canopy.* Garden City, N.Y.: Doubleday, Anchor Books, 1969.

Berger, Peter L., and Luckmann, Thomas. *The Social Construction of Reality.* Garden City, N.Y.: Doubleday, Anchor Books, 1967.

Bonino, José Miguez. *Christians and Marxists.* Grand Rapids, Mich.: Eerdmans, 1976.

————. *Doing Theology in a Revolutionary Situation.* Philadelphia: Fortress Press, 1975.

Brown, Delwin. *To Set at Liberty: Christian Freedom and Human Freedom.* Maryknoll, N.Y.: Orbis Books, 1981.

Brown, Robert McAfee. "The Rootedness of All Theology." *Christianity and Crisis.* July 18, 1977.

————. *Theology in a New Key.* Philadelphia: Westminster Press, 1978.

Bryant, M. Darrol, "Beyond Messianism." *Church and Society,* September/October 1973.

Buber, Martin. *Between Man and Man.* London: Routledge and Kegan Paul, 1947.

Camus, Albert. *The Rebel: An Essay on Man in Revolt.* Trans. Anthony Bower. New York: Vintage Books, 1956.

Capps, Walter Holden. *Hope against Hope.* Philadelphia: Fortress Press, 1976.

Chamberlain, Edward H. *Theory of Monopolistic Competition.* Cambridge, Mass.: Harvard Univ. Press, 1973.

Clark, John Maurice. *Preface to Social Economics.* New York: Farrar and Rinehart, 1936.

Coates, William R. *God in Public: Political Theology beyond Niebuhr.* Grand Rapids, Mich.: Eerdmans, 1974.

Coleman, John. "Civil Religion and Liberation Theology in North

America." In *Theology in the Americas,* ed. Sergio Torres and John Eagleson. Maryknoll, N.Y.: Orbis Books, 1976.

Cone, James H. *Black Theology and Black Power.* New York: Seabury Press, 1969.

————. *A Black Theology of Liberation.* Philadelphia: J. B. Lippincott Co., 1970.

————. *God of the Oppressed.* New York: Seabury Press, 1975.

————. *The Spirituals and the Blues: An Interpretation.* New York: Seabury Press, 1972.

Cormie, Lee. "The Hermeneutical Privilege of the Oppressed: Liberation Theologies, Biblical Faith and Marxist Sociology of Knowledge." *Catholic Theological Society of America Proceedings* 33 (1978):155–81.

Cox, Harvey. *Feast of Fools.* Cambridge, Mass.: Harvard Univ. Press, 1969.

————. *The Seduction of the Spirit.* New York: Simon and Schuster, 1973.

Crites, Stephen. "The Narrative Quality of Experience." *Journal of American Academy of Religion,* vol. 34, no. 3 (1971).

Crosby, Michael H. *Thy Will Be Done.* Maryknoll, N.Y.: Orbis Books, 1977.

Davies, J. G. *Christians, Politics and Violent Revolution.* Maryknoll, N.Y.: Orbis Books, 1976.

Durkheim, Emile. *The Elementary Forms of the Religious Life.* New York: Macmillan Co., 1915.

Dussel, Enrique. *History and the Theology of Liberation.* Maryknoll, N.Y.: Orbis Books, 1976.

Ellacuria, Ignacio. *Freedom Made Flesh.* Maryknoll, N.Y.: Orbis Books, 1976.

Fierro, Alfredo. *The Militant Gospel.* Maryknoll, N.Y.: Orbis Books, 1977.

Galbraith, John Kenneth. *Economics and the Public Purpose.* Boston: Houghton Mifflin, 1973.

————. *The New Industrial State.* New York: Signet, New American Library, 1967.

Greeley, Andrew M. "Civil Religion and Ethnic America." *Worldview,* February 1973.

Harrington, Michael. *The Vast Majority.* New York: Simon and Schuster, 1977.

————. "What Socialists Would Do in America—If They Could." *Dissent,* Fall 1978.

Harris, Seymour E. *American Economic History.* New York: McGraw-Hill, 1961.

Heilbroner, Robert L. *Beyond Boom and Crash.* New York: W. W. Norton, 1978.

————. *An Inquiry into the Human Prospect.* New York: W. W. Norton, 1975.

Held, Virginia. *Property, Profits, and Economic Justice.* Belmont, Calif.: Wadsworth, 1980.

Henderson, Charles P. *The Nixon Theology.* New York: Harper and Row, 1972.

Herzog, Frederick. *Liberation Theology.* New York: Seabury, 1972.

Heschel, Abraham. *Man Is Not Alone.* New York: Farrar, Straus and Young, 1951.

Hodgson, Peter C. *New Birth of Freedom: A Theology of Bondage and Liberation.* Philadelphia: Fortress Press, 1976.

Horvat, Branko, et al., eds. *Self Governing Socialism,* vols. 1 and 2. White Plains, N.Y.: M. E. Sharpe, Inc., 1975.

Horvat, Branko. *The Yugoslav Economic System.* White Plains, N.Y.: M. E. Sharpe, 1976.

Hunsinger, George, ed. and trans. *Karl Barth and Radical Politics.* Philadelphia: Westminster Press, 1976.

The Interpreter's Bible, vol. 5. Nashville, Tenn.: Abingdon Press, 1956.

Jewett, Robert. *The Captain America Complex.* Philadelphia: Westminster Press, 1973.

Jung, Carl G. *Memories, Dreams, Reflections.* New York: Vintage Books, 1963.

Keynes, John Maynard. *The General Theory of Employment, Interest, and Money.* New York: Harcourt, Brace, 1936.

Kohlmeier, Louis M., Jr. *The Regulators.* New York: Harper and Row, 1969.

Krooss, Herman E. and Gilbert, Charles. *American Business*

History. Englewood Cliffs, N.J.: Prentice-Hall, 1972.

Krooss, Herman E. *American Economic Development*. 3rd ed. Englewood Cliffs, N.J.: Prentice-Hall, 1974.

Kuhn, James W. "To Whom and for What Are Business Managers Responsible?" Unpublished paper.

Lehmann, Paul. *The Transfiguration of Politics*. New York: Harper and Row, 1975.

―――. *Union Seminary Quarterly Review* 28, no. 1, 1972.

Lekachman, Robert. *Economists at Bay*. New York: McGraw-Hill, 1976.

―――. *A History of Economic Ideas*. New York: Harper and Row, 1959.

Leontief, Wassily, and McGovern, George. "On Taxing and Redistributing Income." In David Mermelstein, ed., *Economics: Mainstream Readings and Radical Critiques,* 2nd ed. New York: Random House, 1973.

Lowe, Adolph. "Remarks on Receiving the Veblen-Commons Award." In *Journal of Economic Issues* 14 (June 1980).

Marshall, Alfred. *Principles of Economics*. New York: Macmillan, 1920.

Marx, Karl. *Capital*. New York: Modern Library, 1906.

McClelland, David C. *The Achieving Society*. New York: Free Press, 1961.

McDonald, L. "The Energy Tax Act of 1978." *Natural Resources Journal,* October 1979.

McGovern, Arthur F. *Marxism: An American Christian Perspective*. Maryknoll, N.Y.: Orbis Books, 1980.

McLelland, Joseph C. *The Clown and the Crocodile*. Richmond, Va.: John Knox Press, 1970.

Meade, J. E. *The Just Economy*. London: George Allen and Unwin, 1976.

Miranda, José. *Being and the Messiah*. Maryknoll, N.Y.: Orbis Books, 1977.

―――. *Marx and the Bible*. Maryknoll, N.Y.: Orbis Books, 1974.

Moltmann, Jürgen. *The Church in the Power of the Spirit*. New York: Harper and Row, 1977.

———. "A Critical Political Theology of Christians and the Civil Religion of a Nation." Unpublished paper.

———. *The Crucified God.* New York: Harper and Row, 1974.

———. *Religion, Revolution, and the Future.* New York: Charles Scribner's Sons, 1969.

———. *The Theology of Hope.* New York: Harper and Row, 1967.

Nelson, Richard R. *The Moon and the Ghetto.* New York: W. W. Norton, 1977.

Neuhaus, Richard. *Time toward Home.* New York: Seabury, 1975.

Nicol, W. Robertson. *The Expositor's Greek Testament.* Grand Rapids, Mich.: Eerdmans, 1951.

Nouwen, Henri J. M. *Creative Ministry.* Garden City, N.Y.: Doubleday, 1971.

Pachter, Henry. "Freedom, Authority, Participation." *Dissent,* Summer 1978.

Pannenberg, Wolfhart. *Theology and the Kingdom of God.* Philadelphia: Westminster Press, 1969.

Rakowski, James P., and Johnson, J. C. "Airline Deregulation: Problems and Prospects." *Quarterly Review of Economics and Business,* Winter 1979.

Richey, Russel E., and Jones, Donald G., eds. *American Civil Religion.* New York: Harper Forum Books, 1974.

Roberts, J. Deotis. *Liberation and Reconciliation: A Black Theology.* Philadelphia: Westminster Press, 1961.

Robinson, Joan. *Economics of Imperfect Competition.* New York: Macmillan, 1933.

Rosen, Sumner M., ed. *Economic Power Failure: The Current American Crisis.* New York: McGraw-Hill, 1975.

Roszak, Theodore. *The Making of a Counter Culture.* Garden City, N.Y.: Doubleday, Anchor Books, 1969.

Russell, Letty M. *Human Liberation in Feminist Perspective: A Theology.* Philadelphia: Westminster Press, 1974.

Samuelson, Paul A. *Economics.* 9th ed. New York: McGraw-Hill, 1973.

Schumacher, E. F. *Small Is Beautiful: Economics As If People Mattered*. New York: Harper and Row, 1976.

Shaull, Richard. "Introduction to Paulo Freire." In *Pedagogy of the Oppressed*. New York: Seabury, 1973.

Skinner, John. *Prophecy and Religion*. New York: Cambridge Univ. Press, 1951.

Smart, James D. *The Strange Silence of the Bible in the Church*. Philadelphia: Westminster Press, 1970.

Söelle, Dorothee. *Political Theology*. Philadelphia: Fortress Press, 1974.

————. *Suffering*. Philadelphia: Fortress Press, 1975.

Sparks, Jared. *The Library of American Biography*. Vol. 13. Boston: Little, Brown, 1847.

Steiner, George A. *Government's Role in Economic Life*. New York: McGraw-Hill, 1953.

Strain, Charles R. "Ideology and Alienation." *Journal of the American Academy of Religion*, December 1977.

Stringfellow, William. *An Ethic for Christians and Other Aliens in a Strange Land*. Waco, Tex.: Word Press, 1973.

Tillich, Paul. *The Courage to Be*. New Haven, Conn.: Yale Univ. Press, 1952.

————. *Systematic Theology*. 3 vols. Chicago: University of Chicago Press, 1951.

Torres, Sergio, and Eagleson, John, eds. *Theology in the Americas*. Maryknoll, N.Y.: Orbis Boos, 1976.

Turner, Frederick Jackson. *The Frontier in American History*. New York: Holt, Rinehart and Winston, 1920.

Turner, Louis. *Multinational Companies and the Third World*. New York: Hill and Wang, 1973.

Veblen, Thorstein. *The Engineer and the Price System*. New York: Viking Press, 1954.

————. *The Theory of the Leisure Class*. New York: Modern Library, 1931.

————. *The Vested Interests and the Common Man*. New York: Viking Press, 1946.

Walzer, Michael. "Town Meetings and Workers' Control." *Dissent*, Summer 1978.

Weaver, James H., ed. *Modern Political Economy: Radical and Orthodox Views on Crucial Issues*. Boston: Allyn and Bacon, 1973.

Webster's New International Dictionary of the English Language. Springfield, Mass.: G. & C. Merriam Co., 1955.

Wiesel, Elie. *The Gates of the Forest*. New York: Holt, Rinehart and Winston, 1966.

————. *Night*. New York: Hill and Wang, 1960.

Williams, Oliver F., and Houck, John W. *Full Value*. New York: Harper and Row, 1978.

Winquest, Charles E. "The Act of Storytelling and of the Self's Homecoming." *Journal of American Academy of Religion* 42, no. 1 (March 1974).

Woodyard, David O. *Beyond Cynicism: The Practice of Hope*. Philadelphia: Westminster Press, 1972.

Yoder, John Howard. *The Politics of Jesus*. Grand Rapids, Mich.: Eerdmans, 1972.

Zukin, Sharon. *Beyond Marx and Tito: Theory and Practice in Yugoslav Socialism*. New York: Cambridge Univ. Press, 1975.

Index